LISTENING TO
GOD'S WORD

Catholic Spirituality for Adults

General Editor
Michael Leach

Other Books in the Series

Prayer by Joyce Rupp
Reconciliation by Robert Morneau
Holiness by William J. O'Malley
Diversity of Vocations by Marie Dennis
Eucharist by Robert Barron
Mary by Kathy Coffey

LISTENING TO GOD'S WORD

✻

Alice Camille

Maryknoll, New York 10545

Founded in 1970, Orbis Books endeavors to publish works that enlighten the mind, nourish the spirit, and challenge the conscience. The publishing arm of the Maryknoll Fathers and Brothers, Orbis seeks to explore the global dimensions of the Christian faith and mission, to invite dialogue with diverse cultures and religious traditions, and to serve the cause of reconciliation and peace. The books published reflect the views of their authors and do not represent the official position of the Maryknoll Society. To learn more about Maryknoll and Orbis Books, please visit our website at www.maryknollsociety.org.

Manufactured in the United States of America.

Library of Congress Cataloging-in-Publication Data

Camille, Alice L.
    Listening to and proclaiming God's word / Alice Camille.
        p.   cm. – (Catholic spirituality for adults)
    ISBN 978-1-57075-717-4 (pbk. : alk. paper)
    1. Spirituality – Catholic Church. 2. Evangelistic work – Catholic Church.
I. Title.
BX2350.65.C363 2009
248.4'82 – dc22

                                                                    2008034319

In memory of my big brother, Teddy,
who has taught me much
about time and eternity

Contents

Introduction to Catholic Spirituality for Adults   9

Author's Introduction   11

Chapter One
God   23

Chapter Two
World   42

Chapter Three
Story   61

Chapter Four
Crisis   83

Chapter Five
Time   105

Epilogue   125

Introduction to Catholic Spirituality for Adults

C ATHOLIC SPIRITUALITY FOR ADULTS explores the deepest dimension of spirituality, that place in the soul where faith meets understanding. When we reach that place we begin to see as if for the first time. We are like the blind man in the Gospel who could not believe his eyes: "And now I see!"

Catholicism is about seeing the good of God that is in front of our eyes, within us, and all around us. It is about learning to see Christ Jesus with the eyes of Christ Jesus, the Way, the Truth, and the Life.

Only when we *see* who we are as brothers and sisters of Christ and children of God can we begin to *be* like Jesus and walk in his Way. "As you think in your heart, so you are" (Prov. 23:7).

Catholic Spirituality for Adults is for those of us who want to make real, here and now, the words we once learned in school. It is designed to help us go beyond information to transformation. "When I was a child, I spoke as a child, I understood as a child, I thought as a child, but when I became an adult, I put away childish things" (1 Cor. 13:11).

The contributors to the series are the best Catholic authors writing today. We have asked them to explore the deepest dimension of their own faith and to share with us what they are learning to see. Topics covered range from prayer — "Be still, and know that I am God" (Ps. 46:10) — to our purpose in life — coming to know "that God has given us eternal life, and this life is in his Son" (1 John 5:11) — to simply getting through the day — "Put on compassion, kindness, humility, gentleness, and patience" (Col. 3:12).

Each book in this series reflects Christ's active and loving presence in the world. The authors celebrate our membership in the mystical body of Christ, help us to understand our spiritual unity with the entire family of God, and encourage us to express Christ's mission of love, peace, and reconciliation in our daily lives.

Catholic Spirituality for Adults is the fruit of a publishing partnership between Orbis Books, the publishing arm of the Catholic Foreign Mission Society of America (Maryknoll), and RCL Benziger, a leading provider of religious and family life education for all ages. This series is rooted in vital Catholic traditions and committed to a continuing standard of excellence.

Michael Leach
General Editor

Author's Introduction

S HORT BOOKS ABOUT BIG IDEAS run the risk of being
simplistic. But large books risk being confusing, if not
incomprehensible — or worse, unread. So then best to write
short books with big dreams. The only book worth writing is
the one that will be read.

Writing a short book entails trusting the reader. I must have
confidence in you, the unknown companion. I must believe
that your life experience will fill in the blanks I unwittingly
leave behind. I must have faith that the God of my journey is
also the God of yours. This act of faith is the basic creed of
all religious writers. It's especially true of the authors of the
seventy-three books we know as the Bible.

But here I am, talking about trusting you; perhaps you'd
like some reason to trust me. Before we embark on an earnest
journey into the heart of Scripture together, it might help to
know how I got there myself. There are two main ways to
come to the Bible: the easy way and the hard way. Some of
us are just born to do things the hard way.

At age twenty-two, I didn't know there was any other way.
I was desperate. As it happens, desperation is a time-honored
and typical route to the word of God. That's why the Gideons
put all those Bibles in motel rooms. I was a cradle Catholic

from a practicing family, sent to parochial schools and receiving all my sacraments in due season. I certainly had heard enough Scripture in all my years of Mass-going not to be able to plead ignorance. But like many Catholics of that era, I'd never read the Bible for myself. It hadn't been required of me, and I was accustomed to doing what was required. And not a whole lot more.

> *"I'll read it," I found myself vowing fiercely. "I'll read your book, every word of it. Just talk to me. That's the deal. You've got from Genesis until the book of Revelation to talk to me."*

In college, I had a Protestant roommate who read her Bible every evening after supper. I had nothing but admiration for her dedication. But my own Bible, given to me as a high school graduation present by my older sister, remained undisturbed on the shelf. Heaven knows that as an English major I had plenty of long and difficult books to consume every semester as it was. I respected the Bible, but I perceived no need to read it.

When the need arrived, I was quitting graduate school for the second time. I was throwing away the latest of two full-tuition scholarships because of a depression I couldn't shake. I knew these were privileged awards and I was a fool to walk out on them. Yet here I was packing my bags again because the pursuit of knowledge had come to seem pointless and even hopeless. I was having an "Ecclesiastes Moment," but I wasn't biblically astute enough to recognize it.

As I filled up my luggage, I decided to leave behind everything that wasn't absolutely necessary. I wasn't sure where I was going next, so dragging a lot of stuff around was unappealing. I snapped the last suitcase shut and then tossed a few things into the backpack I would be taking on the plane. The Bible my sister had given me was still in the pile of non-essentials that had not made the final cut in this cycle of packing. The sight of it there among the textbooks and toiletries on the bared mattress made my heart ache. I thought I might cry. Instead, I found myself praying.

"So what do you want from me?" I asked, rather testily, of God. "My head hurts from years immersed in the world of ideas. I've read hundreds of books; nothing satisfies. I've absorbed a lot of information but am no wiser. I've passed exams but have no a clue how to live. Forget happiness — that's not even a goal anymore. I'd settle for meaning. I long for a reason to do something, anything." The future yawned so emptily. I literally had no plans beyond getting on that plane and flying back in the direction of my hometown.

The red leather Bible on the bed was gray with dust. Absently I picked it up, meaning only to brush it off. But instead I shoved it into my backpack before I had time to register the thought. "I'll read it," I found myself vowing fiercely. "I'll read your book, every word of it. Just talk to me. That's the deal. You've got from Genesis until the book of Revelation to talk to me."

Over the next two years, I kept my promise. I read that Bible from cover to cover. And God kept the divine promise too. It was one I didn't know had been made, a covenant with those willing to "abide" in this word. Depression lifted. Purpose and meaning became abundant. When I went to school the next time, it was to study the book that had changed my life.

The Journey of the Sacred Authors

Whenever I sit down to write about the Bible — which I do every week as a longtime author of Scripture commentary — I sense a little of what those original authors must have felt. On the one hand, they didn't know they were writing the Bible, as it hadn't been invented yet. During the generations that each was filling up a scroll, and on through the centuries when editors and compilers were reworking and organizing their material, very few of these folks consciously said to themselves: "This is Sacred Scripture, and it's going to be the definitive word on God in every age to come!"

On the other hand, these writers did not regard their work as frivolous. On the contrary, they fervently believed their words reflected the mind of God. Catholic teaching refers to this understanding in terms of *inspiration:* the church holds that the breath of God, that is, the very life of God, is contained in these books. The writer of the Letter to the Hebrews captured this idea when he wrote: "Indeed, the word of God is living and active" (Heb. 4:12).

Whenever I undertake to write about Scripture, I'm struck with the enormity of the task, accompanied by an almost paralyzing sense of humility. This, too, must have been the experience of those first writers. When Isaiah was summoned to his prophetic role, he cried, "Woe is me! I am lost, for I am a man of unclean lips" (Isa. 6:5). If the fellow who composed some of the most beautiful religious language in all of literature deemed himself unworthy of the task, then who am I to attempt to say one word about God?

Yet along with the humility comes the necessity, a compulsion to *ex*press what seems first *im*pressed on the heart. As the prophet Jeremiah described it:

> If I say, "I will not mention him,
> or speak any more in his name,"
> then within me there is something like a burning fire
> shut up in my bones;
> I am weary with holding it in,
> and I cannot. (Jer. 20:9)

In the contest between humility and necessity, the winner is necessity. And this is good news for us, because without such an outcome, we would not have the Bible at all.

And we need the Bible. We need it not just as a record of salvation history but for the sake of what we might call *salvation present*. A living, breathing word has a dynamic relationship with each new generation. This organic dimension of Scripture is built into the design, through the unique collaboration of the writers and the ultimate Inspirer. It's a lovely and generous idea when you think about it. Two great world religions, Judaism and Christianity, owe everything to a long line of writers and editors whose names are largely unknown to us. Patriarchs and prophets, historical chroniclers and Wisdom teachers, Gospel evangelists, epistle writers, and visionaries put together a vast collection of works that are not meant to be a record of the past so much as a discerning look at humanity's present trouble with an eye to the future and its possibilities.

These anonymous or scarcely-less-obscure named writers put down the truths that convicted them in the recesses of their hearts. They did it for the future, for our sake. In their books, large or small, the sacred authors hoped to store for us the revelations they had grasped. They trusted us, the future unknown companions, to unpack their words and to incorporate them into our experience of the world and of God. For they believed that the God of their journey would continue to be the God of ours.

The generosity of the Bible writers impels my own desire to share the Scriptures with others. But it also makes the task of biblical commentary exceedingly hard, because the best book about the Bible has already been written. It's called the Bible. And nothing a commentator writes will be better for the God-seeker to read than that — and perish the thought that someone will read this book *instead* of that one! Yet I still feel the "burning fire in my bones" about writing books like this one. The Bible is an intimidating work for so many that a short book may be the bridge that makes it possible for some to cross over from one to the other.

Crossing Over

There's never a bad time to come to the Bible, to make that crossing. Whenever we get here, we find that we are just in time. The story of God's people always reserves a place for our arrival. It awaits us, like those family Bibles that lay open in a place of honor in many households. The family Bible in my parents' household was of the traditional variety: large, expensively covered, gilt-edged, and thumb-grooved at the start of each book. The words of Jesus, printed in red, blazed across the page like fire. I spent hours as a child looking at the wonderful color plates inside, illustrating privileged moments behind which lay stories I scarcely knew. But to my knowledge no one ever read this book, the red words or the black, until my father picked it up in his seventies. This was the perfect time — after his children were grown, his career ended, and life was more serene — to enter the story.

Yet many of us remain wary of that big book. We know it's a story from long ago, of exotic foreign people, translated from languages most of us don't speak. Even in English, it can sound strangely antique. The approach I initially took — plunging in on page one and persevering through to the last line — is considered a *kamikaze* method by most religious educators. They recommend a kinder, gentler route through the material, starting with the more familiar texts and using a commentary (often available by monthly subscription or written in a page-a-day style) for guidance and instruction. Group study also works well for newcomers, such as attending a parish Bible study that introduces the work thematically, or book by book. Some may want to join a faith-sharing group to reflect on the readings as they come up in the liturgy each Sunday. Those who appreciate the support of a shared journey should consider these avenues, in addition to personal devotional reading.

But there are always those loner folks, like my father and me, who are not "joiners" and will prefer to take this road on their own terms. For this reason I've elsewhere written page-a-day Scripture reflections and survey books that explore the Bible section by section and contribute to serial commentaries for those traveling a more solitary route. In this book, I offer an additional kind of support: an exploration of some of the main themes that permeate Scripture and our own personal stories. If we listen to the Bible with attention to these thematic elements, we may discover how the sacred writers hoped to illuminate our common journey with the light of revelation.

Because this is the goal of reading the Bible: not to learn about ancient Israelites or early Christians, not even to know what God said or Jesus did, but to embrace our own identity as the people of God. If we find our place in the great story of salvation history and can live that out with integrity in salvation present, then we have understood the Bible correctly. Any other interpretation, however scholarly or well intended, is a precious waste of time. The living word of God reaches its fulfillment when it becomes flesh and dwells in us. As in our Eucharist, so in our Bible study.

The purpose of this book, then, is to facilitate that holy crossing from the world of the Bible to the world in which we live and move and have our being. St. Paul uses this same phrase to describe our life in Christ, "For *in him* we live and move and have our being" (Acts 17:28). If our citizenship in the reign of God does not influence our citizenship in this world, we may well be holding a false passport.

Listening to God's Word

If you're a practicing Christian, God's word is practically inescapable. You hear it proclaimed at every worship gathering, in sacramental moments, even at the start of otherwise mundane parish meetings. But hearing is not the same as listening, which our parents were quick to point out every time they asked: "Are you *listening* to me?" They weren't checking our auditory function; what they wanted was obedience, a word rooted in listening. Obedient listening involves offering our attention in order to respond with right action. When we listen to God's word, it's not just to hear the story. It's also to respond by putting the word into practice.

This book is designed to help foster action-oriented listening. Each chapter explores a major Bible theme paralleled with contemporary experiences. Each chapter ends with Scripture citations you can explore, alone or in groups, which illustrate the theme under consideration. Finally, a few short samples of ways to respond attentively are suggested. Throughout the book, I will be quoting from the New Revised Standard Version of Scripture, but I recommend you use the translation most comfortable to you. The best translation is always the one you'll actually read.

One of the most helpful models of responsive listening comes from the story of the prophet Elijah (see 1 Kings 19). After three long years of prophetic ministry in which he was hunted and hated, Elijah was quite ready to retire. He went out to the desert to sit under a broom tree and wait on death. An angel brought him food and water to strengthen him for a journey he was frankly in no mood to take: to the top of the Lord's mountain, Horeb, also called Sinai. Elijah knew well that a trip to Horeb implied an audience with God, like Moses enjoyed before him. Elijah didn't want to talk. Moreover, he didn't want to listen. Listening to God always got him into trouble.

Still, he went. He climbed the mountain and crawled into a cave. We can imagine him there: poor, weary, sad, discouraged Elijah. Nestled in his cave, the predictable theophanies rolled by. Anyone familiar with the story of Moses on Mount Sinai knows how God traditionally makes the divine presence known: a lot of noise, atmospherics, terror, and wonder! But Elijah didn't come out during any of this commotion. God may have spoken to Moses in such cosmic theatrics, but Elijah was too exhausted for this brand of conversation. Finally, the cacophony ends. Elijah hears something described as "sheer silence," sometimes translated as a tiny whispering sound. Respectfully wrapping his face in his cloak, he ventures to the mouth of the cave to encounter his God.

And God apparently honors this approach to the dialogue. Elijah is not reproached for not coming out earlier, or for not responding as Moses might have, or for being discouraged enough to want to die a little while ago under the broom tree.

God seems quite willing to employ many voices to lure the longtime faithful servant out of his hiding place and into the conversation. All Elijah had to do was show up, in reverence and humility, for the encounter to begin.

Here we are, ready to do the same.

Chapter One _____

GOD

"SHOW ME WHAT God looks like." Say this to a group of adults, and you may get no results without further instruction. But the half-dozen children in the room got right to work. I had supplied them with a stack of old magazines and some scissors. The children sat quietly, absorbed in their search, as if they knew precisely what to look for.

I had expected to receive back a half-dozen sunsets and Grand Canyons. After all, isn't creation the most reliable face of God? To be sure, there were some grand vistas in the God collage that emerged. But there were other things, too, surprising images I hadn't anticipated. A young white girl found a picture of an old man with a little boy on his shoulders, both African American. Color did not seem to pose a barrier to her choice. It was also intriguing that many of the pictures were portraits of relationships, as if God could not be imagined in isolation.

Jana was the last to show us her discovery. At thirteen, she was by far the oldest child in the group. She also had Down syndrome. Her size and her unusual perspective often provoked an unsympathetic response from her rowdier peers. When she held up a picture of a smiling young woman in a white gown from a bridal magazine, snickers around the room were audible.

I held up my hand to quiet the others, and asked Jana why she had chosen this image. "Because God is so beautiful!" she exclaimed breathlessly. No one laughed after that.

All these years later, it's hard for me to think of God without that child's definition coming to mind. God is beautiful. This is not merely a romantic notion, but a biblically grounded one. Moses, arguably the most important person in the Hebrew story, once saw God in this way. During the long years of their companionship, Moses once asked if he might be granted a glimpse of the One he served so faithfully. "Show me your glory," Moses pleads in Exodus. God replies that to see the divine face would be fatal for a mortal. But the Lord does agree to reveal the Holy Presence in several concrete ways: "I will make all my goodness pass before you, and will proclaim before you the name, 'The LORD': and I will be gracious to whom I will be gracious, and will show mercy on whom I will show mercy" (Exod. 33:19).

In some translations God's "goodness" is rendered as God's "beauty." To behold divine goodness *is* to apprehend what is truly and infinitely beautiful. This story suggests that the closest we can come to know God is through the contemplation of goodness. We might also understand from this passage that we hear God's name perfectly spoken in acts of divine graciousness and mercy. If we, like Moses, want to see God more clearly, the way to do that is not hidden from us.

Or you can simply trust Jana.

God-Talk for Grownups

God is just about the biggest subject there is. Talking about an Infinite Being could take a while. After twenty-five years of "teaching God" as a religious educator, it's apparent to me that the more we say, the more glaring are the gaps in what remains unsaid. Simplicity helps, and stories work best. The writers of the Bible understood this.

Even if we could cover exhaustively all that's been said about God, we'd find ourselves in the embarrassing position of having spoken only a little of what's true and nothing at all that encompasses the fullness of divinity. God has been defined as perfection, ultimate reality, Ground of Being, the Unmoved Mover responsible for kick-starting the cosmos. To philosophers, God is a "what." To believers, God is a "who." If God is a "who," then God has a story. The story of God naturally precedes all our theology and can never be eclipsed by it.

The Bible is often described to children as the story of God. This is not entirely accurate. The Bible is better understood as the story of God's *people:* the saga of all who view themselves in the mirror of salvation history. God is most certainly a major character in that story, the Best Supporting Actor, so to speak — sometimes compelling the action and sometimes critiquing it, but always hugely invested in what's going on.

Despite the primacy of God to this story, the divine face remains hidden. "No one has ever seen God," John the epistle writer insists (1 John 4:12). The face-to-face encounter eludes humanity, but that's not to say God can't be detected in many tangible and illuminating ways. Nor does it imply that God is hiding from us. In the opening pages of Genesis, God walks in the garden openly in the cool of the evening; it is the man and the woman who choose to hide from the divine presence (Gen. 3:8). If humanity had not originally had something to hide, we can imagine, then seeing God plainly might not be such a fatal proposition now.

Thereafter in the Hebrew story, the Lord is heard but rarely glimpsed. God speaks to Cain before and after the first murder: as in the garden, it's apparent that the scent of our infidelity does not keep God away. Rather, human failure seems to attract an audience with the One who perceives quite well that we need God most when we withdraw from the divine way. God seeks out Noah and his family at the height of humanity's wickedness. Here the divine intention is to save what's still good in the world. God seeks to preserve in creation what most resembles the divine likeness: that essential beauty and goodness. After all, "good" is what God intended for creation and saw in it from the first moment, declaring that goodness seven times, the symbolic number of fullness or completeness (Gen. 1:4, 10, 12, 18, 21, 25, 31).

Already in these first few stories of Genesis, we "see" the essence of God better than any portrait might capture. God is not distant and indifferent, but accessible and involved. God is the ultimate guardian of goodness but also the ready help of sinners. Nonetheless, wicked ways contain the seed of inevitable destruction. Turning away from the source of life is automatically a movement in the direction of death. These aren't stories about a judgmental God. They're cautionary tales about God's high hopes versus humanity's bitter choices.

God Keeps Up the Conversation

Humanity seems to lose interest in the relationship with God as biblical time marches on. The farther we distance ourselves from the way of goodness, the less real God seems all around. It's like moving away from home and then complaining of estrangement from your family. Part of the onus of maintaining the relationship has to come from you.

Consider the traditional tale of the rabbi and the soapmaker who walk into town together. The soapmaker asks the rabbi frankly, "What good is religion, all this talk of God and truth and beauty, when the world is in such a state? See the evil, the suffering, the misery!" The rabbi gives him no answer, and the two walk on together. Eventually they come upon a child playing in the gutter, filthy from head to toe. The rabbi asks the soapmaker, "What good is soap, all these centuries of making and selling and buying it, when this child is so dirty?" The soapmaker objects: "Well, you have to use the soap regularly or it is no good." "Exactly!" the rabbi replies.

Religion is no good if it remains just talk. The story of God cannot be a monologue or it is pointless. Someone must prove willing to listen and to respond. Throughout the Bible, God is willing to keep up the conversation with humanity, but often the Lord is one dialogue partner short. When Abraham arrives on the scene, God discovers someone willing to be responsive. God becomes known to this man and his family through long conversations under starry desert skies, promises made and kept, not to mention one startling ritual of blood. In an entranced state, Abraham encounters divinity passing by in the form of a smoking fire pot and a flaming torch (Gen. 15:17). Hereafter, smoke and fire are signature expressions of God's immanent glory. These elements are repeated in Moses' encounter with the miraculous burning bush, the theophany before the nation at Sinai, and the pillars of cloud and flame that lead the Israelites across the desert. In the Christian story, the divine flame reemerges in the tongues of fire at Pentecost.

The "afterglow" of holy Presence is likewise contagious. Moses must hide his face with a veil after his regular encounters with God in the Tent of Meeting (Exod. 34:29–35). On the mount of Transfiguration, Jesus radiates a white light that makes his face like the sun. Even his clothes become blindingly white (Matt. 17:2; Mark 9:2–3; Luke 9:29).

The image of God as enveloping smoke or cloud also recurs in the Christian story during the baptism of Jesus, the Transfiguration narratives, the "overshadowing" that Mary experiences in the conception of Jesus, and the darkening of the midday sky at Golgotha.

What do we learn about the nature of God through these images? Scripture makes plain that God cannot be seen face-to-face, so God is not fire or cloud any more than the Wizard of Oz might be known by his awe-inspiring mask. Fire and cloud are majestic natural forces that contain the dual potential of death and life. They illuminate and cover, revealing and concealing the nature of God simultaneously. In that sense, they function in a sacramental capacity, participating in the gracious hidden abundance they represent, yet only in the humblest terms. They hint, but never expose.

What we do know from all the stories of God's conversation and self-revelation is that God has never ceased to seek an intimate relationship with us. Far from being enthroned and aloof in some tidy painterly heaven, the divine presence intersects our reality boldly and purposefully in every generation. Who is listening, and responding, in ours?

God and the Word

Attempts to describe God continue to be made. The enterprise of theology is not intended to define God down to manageable terms so much as to create a language by which we can speak about the Ineffable at all. Nineteenth-century theologian Rudolf Otto introduced the phrase *Mysterium Tremendum*. God is "the awe-inspiring mystery" before which we hesitate between fear and wonder. To define God as mystery curiously serves to release God from the confines of definition. Whatever we choose to say about God after that, we've already admitted we can't capture God entirely within our words. This can only be a good thing, because whenever we think we've caught God to our satisfaction, we are doubtless clutching an idol.

A Yiddish proverb declares: "God is an earthquake, not an uncle." The late Rabbi Abraham Heschel used this metaphor not as a summons to dread or timidity before God, but as a call to "radical astonishment" in our spiritual dealings. God the Uncle is a sentimental and predictable character we're tempted to pigeonhole: cranky and eccentric, but ultimately harmless. Organized religion does have the unfortunate side effect of domesticating divinity into nice, safe categories like the church zone, or the morality zone, where God can be both defined and confined. Ancient Israel faced this temptation with the Ark of the Covenant, the Tent of Meeting, and later the northern shrines and the Jerusalem Temple. These places started out as intentional meeting grounds between God and the people, but could just as easily become containers in which to "store" divinity until needed. Is it any wonder that images of God were outright forbidden?

In recalling the "Earthquake God" at Sinai — deftly echoed in Matthew's Gospel with the earthquake following the death of Jesus on the cross — we're cautioned that God will not be anticipated or controlled. Leaving room for radical astonishment reminds us that God is free and will not "behave" for us according to any preestablished rules we might lay down. It also leaves room for hope, for without a fervent respect for God's liberty to break the rules, our hope can only be diminished or extinguished by "the facts" in any given situation. "The facts" tell us only what is presently true or likely in the future. They cannot predict what actually will happen, for the God of perfect liberty is the God of the impossible (Matt. 19:26; Mark 10:27; Luke 1:37).

We see this respect for divine freedom in the Hebrew response to the Holy Name. Moses specifically asks God to reveal the divine Name at the site of the burning bush. But ever afterward, the Jewish community is notoriously reluctant to speak the Name aloud. The power of naming is part of the stewardship God gives to the first human being in the creation account. To name something means to exercise authority over it, something Israel will not presume to do with God. YHWH, often translated as "I AM WHO I AM" (Exod. 3:14), is also rendered in the Torah as "I WILL BE WHAT I WILL BE" — leaving open the essential mystery of God to be revealed in each new encounter.

God the Uncle is a sentimental and predictable character we're tempted to pigeonhole: cranky and eccentric, but ultimately harmless.

The traditional theological parameters for God are "all-powerful, all-knowing, and ever-present." Trying to stuff Infinity into a box, even a verbal one, is a useless and possibly dangerous way to begin if the results limit our religious imagination and expectations. As Thomas Aquinas wryly noted, "The most we can know is that we do not know God." Aquinas composed more smart words about divinity than most of us will ever read, and yet he was frank in admitting the limitations of our God-talk.

Christians have learned to speak of the boundlessness of God through the medium of love: "Whoever does not love does not know God, for God is love" (1 John 4:8). If it's possible to behold a Beatific Vision in this lifetime, it might be

in the face of someone we love. Love is the most expansive
experience we know. It makes heroes out of ordinary people
and gives meaning and purpose to the bleakest and most desperate existence. Love is a cornucopia of virtues expressed
in many ways, as St. Paul tells us in the First Letter to the
Corinthians. But above all, "love never ends" (1 Cor. 13:8).
Though prophecy, language, and knowledge reach their limits
and fail us, love pushes on to the ultimate horizon and brings
us into the presence of God.

God *Is* the Word

I once heard a story about a child in a disadvantaged neighborhood. He used to sit on the stoop at the convent and draw
pictures for the Sisters. One Sister, admiring his drawings,
asked him, "Do you like art, Ronnie?"

"What's art?" the boy asked. He drew, but he did not know.

So the Sister showed him a book full of paintings by El
Greco and Renoir and Matisse and Van Gogh. And ever after
that, Ronnie called himself an artist.

Sometimes the right word has the power to name us, or
even to save us. As the story goes, God the artist once created everything out of words alone. "Let there be light," the
divine words boomed into the void. And light emerged at the
sound of its name. John's Gospel tells us that the Word was
with God before all else that is (John 1:1–3). As noted earlier,
even when God no longer walked openly in the garden of the
world with us — because we no longer walked with God, it
should be said — God did not grow silent. The divine word

that invented a good world kept talking even after we, on the whole, stopped listening.

And because we would not listen, we forgot who we were. We forgot we were "good." We no longer saw the divine likeness when we looked in the mirror, but became simply self-absorbed. Eventually, we drowned out the voice of God until it may as well have been silent. Yet God continues to pronounce special words of promise in the stories of covenant with Noah, Abraham, Moses, and David. Unlike human words that can be thin and deceitful, God's words are as substantial and binding as the matter and energy that formed the world. They shine with the beauty of divine goodness, and are demonstrated with acts of graciousness and mercy. Over and over, humanity fails to respond in kind.

In these biblical stories, God speaks often in the language of law. To modern ears, law may imply cold and distant authority, legalism, and rigidity. But in Hebrew, law means "guiding light." It's an offer of help rather than a leaden obligation. In a great tribute to the wonderful nature of divine law, the psalmist speaks of it as a "lamp to my feet and a light to my path" (Ps. 119:105). God's willingness to spell out good choices and harmful ones according to the divine perspective was an invitation to intimacy and a tremendous honor. Needless to say, humanity largely ignores these words too.

The divine voice is heard next in the oracles of the prophets. Almost continually for six hundred years, prophets from Elijah to Joel announced a "word of the LORD" to the people of God. These men — and sometimes women like Deborah in Judges, Huldah in 2 Kings, and later Anna in Luke's Gospel — claimed the authority to speak on behalf of God. Their good words were often spurned, yet the prophets persistently put their lives at risk to raise God's voice above the din of politics, commerce, and sometimes even religion.

After the time of the prophets, for a few centuries the sages of the Wisdom tradition governed the God-talk. The writers of books like Job and Ecclesiastes, Proverbs, Sirach, and Wisdom all sought to keep the conversation going. They did not claim the authority of the prophets to speak God's word directly. Rather, they imitated the practice of foreign Wisdom schools and embraced reason and observation to tease out the mystery of God's ways.

Then, as Christianity tells the story, God's Word became flesh and moved into the neighborhood (John 1:14). From then on, for those who believe, the conversation would take place on very different terms.

Goodness in Our Likeness

Looking for God? Chances are one of the last places you'd look is in a human face. It's easy to catch a glimpse of the Divine in a sparkling nighttime sky or pounding green-blue ocean surf. Cathedral groves of old-growth trees and plunging rocky gorges may bring you to your knees in praise. So too the art and architecture of great masters can make the soul fly upward. But the actual men and women around us are, for the most part, not a particularly inspiring lot. Sharing our nature, they also harbor our faults to a greater or lesser extent. In the quest for God, we tend to seek elsewhere than our own fallible and disappointing kind.

All of which means that sometimes we will miss God born into a minority race to a rather questionable couple of humble means. We won't notice God slumbering in a makeshift crib, reaching across a table for bread, or walking weary and barefoot down a road. We won't see God waiting for our hospitality, talking to the wrong kind of folks, touching people with disgusting illnesses, championing those who have been publicly disgraced, breaking rules in order to obey a greater law, denouncing religion that is self-serving and self-satisfied. We won't recognize that it's God over there being abandoned by friends. We won't see God condemned and alone, suffering, humiliated, and dying.

But if we have listened to the story of Jesus and we believe that the Divine Word has lived in our midst as one of us, then we know that the primary place to look for God is in our sisters and brothers. "Truly I tell you, just as you did it to one of the least of these who are members of my family, you did it to me" (Matt. 25:40).

Not long ago I took an unusual route home through the town where I live. Even in a small community, there can be streets you seldom travel out of convenience or preference. On this unfamiliar route, I passed one of those neglected yards that signal poverty or distress. Inside the yard was a lopsided wooden table with a hand-printed sign propped up against a box. I don't know how I even noticed the sign; it was so ill designed to get attention. But I could see the box clearly, heaped with grapefruit from the tree just behind it. The day was hot, the yard had neither fence nor dog, and the fruit lured me in to read what was on the sign. "Five for a dollar," it said. The fruit looked fresh and beautiful, and the price was an absurd fraction of what the store was currently charging. I was incredulous.

So I went to the battered screen door, put my face close, and called inside. After a little shuffling, an old woman in a worn housedress came to the door with a plastic bag, which she handed to me with a radiant smile. I gave her two dollars. She let me pick ten of the best pieces of the shimmering fruit, all the while bursting with delight that she had two dollar bills in her hand. I knew the fruit was worth ten dollars, for crying out loud. I wanted to give her more money. It was clear from the look of her property that she could use it.

As I turned to go, the woman glanced out to the road and realized I did not have a car. "Are you walking?" she asked, anxious for me. "It's not far," I assured her. She reached into her box again and gave me two more pieces of fruit. "For your trouble," she said.

At that point, I was ready to weep. I took her in my arms and hugged and blessed her. "Thank you," she said, as happily as if I had stuffed the pockets of her housedress with cash. I left with my arms full of fruit and a heart brimming with gratitude for a generosity that was unfathomable.

The God of the Incarnation is like this, setting up a sign in an obscure location and waiting on passersby to discover it. All are welcome; few will even take this road; fewer will stop and venture near. But for those who do, there is unreasonable bounty. It reminds us of Wisdom's table set for all comers (Prov. 9:1–6), or the invitation issued in prophecy, "Ho, everyone who thirsts, come to the waters; and you that have no money, come, buy and eat!" (Isa. 55:1). It cannot help but remind us of the meals Jesus shares with terribly unlikely people, food sometimes miraculously multiplied on hillsides or gathered in nets that were empty moments ago. It's the fish frying on the beach for hungry fishermen, or tables set with tax collectors and notorious women in mind. When God becomes one of us, then God is most certainly coming to dinner and is even more likely the host at the feast.

God: Invested, Incarnate, Indwelling

If we listen attentively to the stories of the Bible, we see the infinite beauty of God regularly revealed in episodes of divine goodness. When we move from the Hebrew story to the Christian story, God's goodness is manifest in the life, work, and teachings of Jesus. That the Divine Word enters human history is itself cause for radical astonishment. What does it mean for the Creator to endure the limitations of creation? St. Paul compares this self-emptying act of divine charity as taking on the form of a slave (Phil. 2:5–7). Consider that God, who could say anything at all and have the Divine Word instantly obeyed, spoke this word instead into the womb of a Hebrew girl in an occupied country. The eternal God stepped into a moment of time, locked into the linear push of history. The infinite God became a human, a baby, a male, a Jew. The Omnipotent One would be subjected and bound to a cross. The Omniscient would wonder if he'd been forsaken.

Divine goodness is on display in the daily ministry of Jesus as well. We can see it in the miraculous interventions, the healing of helpless, hopeless people. But it's just as evident in the beautiful words of teaching, a new "guiding light" offered to lost sheep without a shepherd. Divine goodness shares a conversation with a much-married Samaritan woman at a well, or a Canaanite mother who insists that the needs of her sick daughter are more important than any Grand Plan. Divine goodness breaks the Sabbath rest so that human beings for whom that rest was inaugurated can know peace. Jesus talks to anyone, men and women, insiders and outsiders, religious leaders and sinners. The conversation takes place in word and deed, from the crib to the cross and beyond the grave.

The conversation doesn't end when Jesus ascends and is lost from view. Divine goodness passes the baton again in the events of Pentecost. Now if you want to see the beauty of God at work in the world, you have only to look to the disciples. They take on the "shine" of God every bit as much as Moses once did — only instead of an outward glow, they radiate the power of the indwelling Spirit. This Spirit is the guiding principle of the burgeoning church. Teaching, healing, and liberation remain the familiar signs of divine authority being spoken into the world. If you want to see God in the world today, trace the paths of those who carry this light forward. Review the lives of the saints and heroes who do what Jesus did: surrendering their advantage for the sake of those with no advantage, bringing light, healing, and liberation where it is needed.

If the Bible tells the story of God, then this is the story it tells. We call this threefold movement of God's goodness as perceived in salvation history by the name "Trinity." Theologians talk about the nature of God as "unity-in-community," a dynamic interior relationship rather than a static monolith of Being like the lonely self that so preoccupies us. When God uses the royal "we," Trinity isn't kidding. I think of the children I mentioned earlier in this chapter, who cut up magazines searching for images of God. So many of those pictures were of relationships rather than isolated figures. I don't think the kids knew much if anything about trinitarian theology. But they did intuit that a Love this big could not be expressed in isolation.

Before we finish a regrettably short survey on the story of God, let's have a story about those who show us how to come into the presence of Unity-in-Community. A visiting children's choir performed one Sunday at our parish. The courage of those youngsters standing in a semicircle on risers behind the altar touched our hearts as much as their musical selections. In front of them stood their director, a young woman whose back was to the assembly. She waved her arms to the beat of the songs, making cupped gestures with her hands that the children followed as meaningfully as sign language. At the end of the final verse, the director pointed right up to the ceiling, her arm an arrow of urgency, one finger touching heaven. As a group, those children struggled upward for the high note, following that finger almost bodily in the effort. Some made it. Most didn't. But all went as far as they could, and the results were pleasing to the assembly and, we might think, to the Lord.

The choir director, whose face we never saw, reminded me of God, calling us to harmony with the divine will and with one another, using every sign possible to bring us into unison. The motivating pointed finger is not always the same: it might be the ancient law or the teachings of the church. It could be a sacramental sign, a beloved face, the yearning need of the poor, or the voice of our conscience. Sometimes the finger of God points at our hearts through a moving story we see at the movies or read in a book — or live in the course of an average afternoon. Despite our efforts to follow that finger, many of us won't reach the perfection of that high note. It may be beyond our frail humanity to arrive there. But the goal is still to follow as far and as nearly as we can. The rest, we understand, will be forgiven.

Read, Explore, Discuss

Genesis 1: Divine goodness in creation

Exodus 37: Moses sees God's beauty

Isaiah 55: An invitation to God's presence

Psalms 19 and 119: God in creation and in law

Proverbs 9: Wisdom issues her call

John 1: The Word becomes flesh

Philippians 2:1–18: Adopting the mind of Christ

Acts of the Apostles 2: The Spirit in the church

Galatians 5:22–23: Good fruits of the Spirit in us

In the Spirit of Responsive Listening

◆ Enter the conversation with God through prayer, contemplation, and Scripture reading.

◆ Praise the God of creation by taking refreshment in natural surroundings. Exercise stewardship of the environment personally and politically.

◆ Encounter the God of incarnation in relationships of love, generosity, and respect. Seek illumination, healing, and liberation for yourself, and for others both near and far.

◆ Invite the God of the indwelling Spirit to guide you in all your ways.

Chapter Two

WORLD

THE WORLD IS A MESS. Our individual lives are messy. The world is also undeniably a graced and blessed place. Our lives are likewise graced and blessed beyond measure. How do we hold two conflicting realities together in one place? How do we live the hope implicit in the blessing while the messy side of reality is dashing those hopes at every turn?

If God is the first character to appear in the Bible, "the world" is a close second. From its inception as a divine work, the nature of the world is declared good. But hardly does the story of the world begin before that unqualified goodness is challenged by temptation. The world undergoes a devolution once sin enters the picture. The rot sets into creation, and death is not merely a possibility but an inevitability for every living thing.

But is it right to say that the world, originally infused with divine goodness, turns evil? Certainly evil is now rooted as an ever-present option in a theater of free choosers. Catholic teaching holds that original sin casts such a long shadow on human history that every baby yet to be born is subject to its chill from the first moment of life. None of us, in this sense, can speak of our innocence. In a realm governed by the effects of original sin, all citizens of the earth are guilty and condemned to die before they take their first breath.

Presumptive guilt is hardly an encouraging premise on which to build our self-understanding. It would mean living out our entire lives on death row awaiting the fulfillment of our sentence. If we're born for destruction, despair would seem the only reasonable orientation to life. This is why some theologians prefer to inaugurate the discussion of human reality not with original sin but with the notion of original blessing. God blesses each aspect of the created order in its first hour and calls it good, without qualification or exception. To share in that goodness is our original purpose. Whatever transpired after that initial hour does not detract from what God has had in mind for all of creation before the world began. And God's will is never thwarted, as prophecy tells us:

So shall my word be that goes out from my mouth;
it shall not return to me empty,
but it shall accomplish that which I purpose,
and succeed in the thing for which I sent it.

(Isa. 55:11)

If prophecy is to be trusted, then we can set our minds at rest on this score: God's intentions for the creation bearing the stamp of divine goodness have not changed.

Sin may issue its implicit death sentence, but there is a trump card for the effects of sin and even death. That, too, will come through the created order according to God's unfailing purposes.

Who Are We?

In the previous chapter, we addressed the question: Who is God? Our answer had many parts, but a major component in all of them is that God is the Creator who seeks relationship with creation. God is the initiator of the conversation, our never-ending dialogue partner. God wants to tell us something, and it must be an urgent message for the Supreme Being to chase us down the long centuries of history to deliver it. Within the Judeo-Christian tradition, we have come to speak of this pursuit as the urgent quest of the Lover for the beloved. Love never ends. It doesn't give up no matter how many times it is rebuffed. Love won't take no for an answer. It lives in joyful anticipation of the day when the beloved turns at last and says, with unreserved surrender to love's possibilities, "Yes!"

What makes the beloved flee the presence of Love in the first place? It has to do with the story of the world, what we might call our communal backstory. Knowing who we are helps us to locate ourselves in relationship to the God who seeks us. The trouble in the world as we know it might be traced to the fact that most of us have no idea who we are and were created to be in the first place.

A friend recounted to me a wonderful vignette about her three-year-old granddaughter. The little girl was sitting on the floor with paper and crayons, very absorbed in the business of creating. Her mother asked her what she was doing. Without looking up or interrupting her work, the girl replied, "I am being myself."

I am regularly convinced that if you want to know anything about God, don't ask a theologian. Find a child! Jesus went on record saying that to enter the reign of God we have to become like children. I fervently wish I could say with as much integrity and simplicity as that child did that I am, in any given moment, being myself. The best I can often say is that I am struggling and striving to *become* myself, that is, to become the person God intended me to be at my inception. I'm working on it — but I'm tempted at every turn to become someone quite unlike my true self, a deformity that denies original goodness, beauty, and love in favor of their opposites.

God is most certainly like that child in being the Divine Self, or "Being Itself" as theologian John McQuarry has phrased it. The name of God, the unadorned and unqualified "I AM," claims much more than I do when I say, "I am from Pennsylvania" or "I am Catholic." God isn't being any one thing or playing one role — Creator, Saving Power, Almighty, or Father — so much as purely and ultimately Being. This eternal, vital present tense has no Alpha or Omega. God isn't pressing on through time, space, and events like we do, making the divine way toward some deliberate destination. God has arrived, or we might say, is arriving all the time. But more on that idea in the final chapter.

To say that God is absolute Being means that, while we can discuss the divine attributes — qualities that belong to God and direct us God-ward when we encounter them in our experience — we know these are merely elements of the Sacred and not the whole truth. Beauty, goodness, love, wisdom, glory, justice, holiness, and many other aspects of divinity can be discovered in our world, but they are always partial, marred by the reality of our broken condition, seen "in a mirror dimly" (1 Cor. 13:12) and never in their fullness. Yet we know that, as creatures bearing the divine image, we were made to be like God and to be with God so that Love might find its fulfillment. As God is, we are meant to be. However far we presently stand from reflecting the attributes of God, that's how far we are from being who we really are — and who we long to be, if we pay attention to the passion that stirs in our hearts when we catch a glimpse of that image in others.

To speak of our true identity, therefore, is bigger than saying "I am [any one thing]." It is enough, as my friend's granddaughter knows, to sit on the floor *simply being,* without further explanation or defense. But consider also what the child is doing. She is drawing, creating. She knows herself and is being herself in the context of imaginative invention. Since our story of God in the Bible begins with the fashioning of the world, we can know nothing of divine existence apart from this fundamental creativity. Our first experience of God is creation. To say we are made in God's likeness, then, means on some primary level that we are made to participate in the activity of creating and producing. Is it any wonder we experience our happiest hours when we exercise that aspect of our being: cooking, singing, hammering, gardening, writing a poem, raising a family?

To Create or to Destroy?

In the creation account, God and the world are initially on the same page, full of life, goodness, and creativity. "Be fruitful and multiply" is our first commission (Gen. 1:22, 28). Before long, however, the world's free choosers turn their creative potential toward destruction. They move from love toward isolation, from unity to division, from life toward death. Soon, the first couple is not only alienated from their Creator, but also from each other in the blame game that ensues. They are separated adversarially from the rest of creation as they've known it in the benevolent garden. Now, obeying the call to be fruitful and multiply will be fulfilled in pain. The generative aspect of our humanity is ever after complicated by suffering — as every parent, artist, farmer, pastor, carpenter, and inventor is quick to admit. L'Arche founder Jean Vanier, in his book *Community and Growth: Our Pilgrimage Together,* described our creative efforts by noting, "Every child commits a violence when it is born." If bringing forth life from the womb is difficult and costly, coaxing life from the ground will be frustrating and laborious as well. Humanity will dig in the earth until each man and woman finally and exhaustedly returns to it. "Remember you are dust," the sign of Ash Wednesday dolorously declares. In the frustrations and humiliations we experience each day in the world, our "dustiness" is frankly hard to forget.

Much is made of the first sin in Genesis. The decision not to listen to God is so enormous and consequential that it enables every sin thereafter. It's as if we, offered a partnership in the divine conversation, chose to talk to the devil instead. That other insinuating voice in our ear has had our attention ever since, and it's hell-bent on destruction. The voice of deceit lures us away from our true nature at every opportunity. We wander off in the direction of "deadly" choices as the church describes them in the list of capital sins — pride having primacy of place among them.

The second sin recorded in the Bible is fratricide. Cain slays his brother, Abel. This dreadful act seems far worse than what Adam and Eve did; yet if we're paying attention, this second deed is the natural consequence of the first. Turn from life and you embrace death. Turn from love and enter hate. Stop listening to the Creator and tune in to the destroyer. Sin is a contagion that spreads and worsens; a stain that deepens; a rot that eats through everything in time. But we also see that sin works in concert with itself as efficiently as the world's original harmony once did. Cain's sin of fratricide is predicated by other deadly sins: envy, anger, and pride. As the teachings of Jesus will later make plain, the sin that starts in the heart ends all too often in the deed (Matt. 5:21–48).

The third biblical sin is casually reported. A man murders another for striking and wounding him (Gen. 4:23); does anyone even notice anymore how glaringly horrible such violence is? The outrageous choice for sin has become normalized. In a few short chapters, the world has devolved from the innocence of Eden to a comfortably domestic relationship with wickedness. Lamech, the second murderer, composes what appears to be a little ditty about his deed to inform his wives.

Not many more generations pass till the time of Noah, when the world is literally awash in evil.

Meanwhile, where's God in all this? The writers of Genesis are clear that God suffers these events intimately. God rushes in to make clothes for Adam and Eve the moment their nakedness shames them. God warns Cain in advance of the Tempter's nearness and encourages him to master it. God seeks Cain out when guilt and fear overwhelm him and gives him a protective mark to preserve — not to condemn — his life. By Noah's generation, when the world is totally governed by sin, God demonstrates nothing but anguish: "The LORD saw that the wickedness of humankind was great in the earth, and that every inclination of the thoughts of their hearts was only evil continually. And the LORD was sorry that he had made humankind on the earth, and it grieved him to his heart" (Gen. 6:5–6).

God's anguish at the world's sinful state is recognizable again in the hour that Jesus mounts the cross. God's participation in human suffering cannot be more complete. How curious, then, that some of us persist in carrying an image of a distant God who must be obeyed under threat of punishment. The biblical God suffers each mortal wrongdoing most personally and seeks always to restore what is lost by it.

Lost in the Chaos

The name Dwight Leeray may not ring a bell in the roll call of the saints. He was not, in the usual sense, a martyr for his faith, not an Oscar Romero or Martin Luther King Jr., defending dangerous truths against an offending world. Dwight was just a guy hustling spare change in front of a bank in downtown Berkeley. He was a fellow routinely rebuffed and ignored as he held out a Styrofoam cup while standing the legally required number of paces from the ATM. Those of us in the neighborhood didn't know his name until after he was dead. We just called him the God-Bless-You Guy.

Because that's what Dwight did all day long, just blessed people as they came down the sidewalk. He never asked for money. He blessed us all in the name of God and wished us a nice day. In November he urged us to vote even though he, without a registered domicile, did not share that privilege. In May and December, he wished students laden with backpacks success with their final exams, though he hadn't had much formal education. He blessed us and cheered us on in every season and endeavor of our lives, as if the victory of one meant victory for all. Until the night, that is, when someone beat him up for the money in his cup. The thief got two dollars. Dwight died of his injuries.

The newspaper carried no picture of Dwight for us to know that the story of the murder was about him. But the headlines announcing the death of the "God-Bless-You Guy" instantly brought that familiar fellow to mind. We had never known his name or where he came from, where he slept or why he stood on the same corner day after day with his humble cup. We knew him solely as a conduit of blessing. No one stands on the corner by the ATM to bless us now.

The story of sin in the world often sounds like this. It's jarring and erratic and pointless. It makes no sense because there is no sense in it. When we stop to ponder the first eleven chapters of Genesis — which cover Adam and Eve, Cain and Abel, the Great Flood, and the Tower of Babel — we are aghast that so much was forfeited for so little. It's as if the divine blessing implicit in the world is kicked aside for the sake of two dollars in change. History is full of wars fought, cities burned, and lives squandered with the bizarre conviction that victory could ever be pronounced over such tragedy. Meanwhile the so-called victors stand in the rubble of history and pocket the change.

Humanity's estrangement from its original goodness is an aching reality in every generation. The biblical writers trace our descent into this mess with simple lines: alienation from God leads to alienation between genders, brothers, neighbors, until everyone is both stranger and enemy. At the site of Babel, humanity literally loses its common language, and along with it any vestige of unity. See what comes of walking out on the conversation with God: now we can't even talk to each other.

This, biblically speaking, is chaos. It is no neutral condition but a lawlessness that echoes the state of things before the divine activity of creation: "The earth was a formless void and darkness covered the face of the deep" (Gen. 1:2). If it sometimes feels like there's no escaping the Genesis story, that you're constantly forced to double back and deal with it, you're onto something. Genesis is placed at the head of the Bible, but it functions curiously as a summation of sorts. It is actually the last book written of the crucial unit of five works known as the Pentateuch, or in Hebrew *Torah*. Genesis was designed to contextualize and explain why the world is as it is. Before God organizes and defines creation, we're told, the "formless void and darkness" prevailed. Theologically, we say the world was created *ex nihilo* — out of nothing. But the Bible describes this "nothing" as a black hole of meaning that lacks all proper restraint. Primordial chaos is innately senseless. God speaks purpose and reason into the organization of the world when each aspect of creation is pronounced "good" on arrival. This is what the world is for: to mirror and to participate in divine goodness.

The choice to do otherwise — to use good things for bad purposes — perverts the world's design. Creation is, so to speak, broken in its fall. Primordial chaos seeps back in through the cracks of imperfection now widening everywhere. This senselessness and lack of restraint is the precise opposite of what God infused into creation. Chaos has surely made a comeback, and we see it everywhere in the news: in countries with ever-revolving dictatorships, in refugee camps and slums, in families without responsible grownups in charge, and in communities large and small lacking genuine leadership. Lawlessness — the absence of the "guiding light" in Hebrew terms — can even be detected in the individual soul that has no informed conscience to follow. How many people do we know who seem to wander aimlessly through life, unable to hold marriages together, keep jobs, or develop a coherent sense of what it is they are about? In an environment of chaos, with no clear map to guide us, one route may seem as good as another.

Making Sense of the World

I remember a season of my life when I was sad for a long time. No matter what happened to me during that period, I could not seem to make my way back to joy. A friend came to encourage me and asked: "What's the bottom line? What do you believe in, when you doubt everything else?"

The question caught me by surprise. But I was more surprised to find that I had an immediate answer. "I believe in the mercy of God," I said. To the depths of my soul, I knew I could count on that. The conscious recognition of that certainty gave me courage to keep on walking to the end of the sadness. In a world overwhelmed by the shadow of death and surrendered to chaotic forces, it's easy to forget that a bottom line is out there.

Biblical writers of the Wisdom tradition struggled to find a bottom line to the dark forces at work in the world. Through the character of Job, they explored the injustice in human suffering, the depth of mortal anguish, and the apparent silence of God on the matter. If goodness is not rewarded and evil is permitted to have its day at the expense of the innocent, then what difference does it make how we live?

Job is not as fortunate in his circle of friends as I am, according to the story. His comforters make a mess of their attempts to console and advise. They are glued to the worldview that divine justice guarantees the prosperity of the just and the punishment of the wicked. Since Job has lost his children, his wealth, and his health, he's apparently done something wrong. They don't know what it might be; they admit Job may not even be aware of his offense. But that doesn't matter: he ought to repent and beg forgiveness anyway.

Job is appalled by this suggestion, as he should be. It makes God as arbitrary and unfair as the world itself. If evil and suffering are the result of personal guilt, then Job has been judged wrongly and he demands a retrial. If punishment retroactively imparts guilt, then God is absurd. If guilt and suffering have no meaningful relationship, then the world is reduced to randomness and despair. Job stares into the void of his desperate situation and wants someone to make sense of it. The only one who can do this is the One who created the world in the first place.

If the point of the book of Job is to supply a reason for why good people suffer, then the work is a failure. What Job does get for his pains is the audience with God he demanded all along. The Lord replies to Job for four chapters straight — God's longest soliloquy in Scripture. God takes this opportunity to describe the world to Job as it was intended to be: full of wonder and delight, beauty, complexity, and subtlety. God says nothing at all about evil and suffering. Frankly, God says nothing about humanity and what has become of the world under its stewardship.

Job becomes a privileged participant in the divine conversation. While God does not explain his suffering, nor is Job blamed for what has befallen him. Unwilling to repent sins he did not commit, in the end Job is willing to repent one thing: his ignorance. That a signed confession of mortal ignorance comes out of the Wisdom tradition is a marvel in itself. Perhaps the first stage of wisdom is to know, as Thomas Aquinas said, that we do not know God.

Another Wisdom writer took aim at the apparent absurdity of the world in Ecclesiastes. While Job represents the voice of faithful dissent in a world gone wrong, the speaker in Ecclesiastes is considerably more cynical in his dismissal of mortal existence as not merely unjust but pointless. An early editor adds an epilogue to the book that retreats considerably from the speaker's original conclusions: "Fear God, and keep his commandments; for that is the whole duty of everyone" (Eccles. 12:13). This thin veil pulled over a brutally honest protest fooled no one, as the sages continued to argue against including Ecclesiastes in the Bible for several centuries. As one wrote, such books "did not make the hands pure." It may be impossible to consider the messy realities of the world without getting the hands a little dirty.

The World, Our Adversary

A fourteen-year-old girl named Annemarie once confided to her mother that she knew exactly what she wanted to do after high school. She would enroll in a music school and become a composer. To Annemarie's disappointment, her mother remained silent in response to her declaration. At dinner that night, however, Annemarie's mother said, "Tell your father what you told me this afternoon about your plans." Annemarie repeated her goal: to study music and become a composer. Unexpectedly, her father hauled off and struck her across the face, almost knocking her out of her chair.

"You will finish high school and get a job with the phone company," her father said firmly, "and you will work there until you retire and get your pension." The matter was dropped; Annemarie finished high school and went to work for the phone company. And as her father had outlined, she remained there until retirement and drew a good pension. By then Annemarie's parents had died. So the woman, now in her sixties, took her pension and enrolled in a music school. And she began at last to compose music.

In a broken world, the divine likeness embossed in each of us may seem to have vanished altogether. But it's there, just as the composer lived in Annemarie until it had the chance to emerge. Many biblical psalms bulge with praise for the goodness of the world still evident, despite the horror of human injustice. Other psalms express confidence that God will rule with justice in due season. Every saving act in Scripture testifies to God's presumption that the world is worth saving and can be salvaged, even at this late hour.

The tragedy of human history is that so much goodness implicit in the world is lost to oppressive and death-dealing forces like Annemarie's uncomprehending father. The good news is that Annemaries everywhere remain in possession of their inner composer and can summon it into being in a more fruitful hour. How much time and opportunity is squandered in our lives may be subject to factors beyond our control. But often all that's lacking is the courage to say no to oppressive forces — to the "culture of death," as Pope John Paul II often designated those powers — and to claim the creative spirit of goodness that is our birthright as the children of God.

Until such time, the world remains an ambiguous character in the Bible. Late New Testament writers were very suspicious of the material realm, as was the Greek philosophical tradition swirling around them. The writings that emerged from what's known as the Johannine community — John's Gospel, the letters of John, and the book of Revelation — are uniquely concerned with the irreconcilable differences between life in the world versus life in Jesus, which is definitively "not of this world" (John 18:36). The opening of John's Gospel, "In the beginning," consciously imitates the style of Genesis to recall that ancient story, and the Gospel presents the ghost of that fallen world as its greatest antagonist. The character of the world is never so dynamically portrayed as in this Gospel, where it is referred to nearly sixty times.

In a broken world, the divine likeness embossed in each of us may seem to have vanished altogether. But it's there, just as the composer lived in Annemarie until it had the chance to emerge.

To the Johannine writers, the world is blind to the truth embodied in the Word of God: "He was in the world, and the world came into being through him; yet the world did

not know him" (John 1:10). This ignorance does not affect
the plan, thankfully: "For God so loved the world that he
gave his only Son, so that everyone who believes in him may
not perish but may have eternal life" (3:16).

Jesus is the Lamb of God who takes away the sin of the
world (John 1:29); he is deliberately sent into the world for
this purpose and is the world's savior (4:42), prophet (6:14),
bread (6:33), and light (8:12). Jesus comes to judge the world
(9:39), to be sure, but not to condemn it (3:17; 12:46–47).
Still, those whose deeds are conformed to evil will prefer the
darkness of the world to the light of Jesus (3:19).

How sad it is to consider that the world, once spoken into
being by the word of God, is now antagonistic toward the
Incarnate Word come to rescue it! The hatred of the world
for its one true hope is startlingly reiterated across the pages
of John's Gospel and the letters of John as well (see especially
John 7:7; 15:18–25; 1 John 3:13). There's an unbridgeable
conflict between those who are "of the world" and those
who choose not to belong to it (John 8:23). The only es-
cape from the world is to "hate" it in return (12:25). Those
who belong to Jesus are "chosen out of the world" — and
hated by the world as a result (15:19). Those who remain
loyal to the world cannot receive the Spirit of truth (14:17),
nor can they acquire the peace that Jesus alone can give
(14:27).

This ferocious battle between the world and its Savior extends to the Father of Jesus as well: those who hate Jesus hate
his Father (15:23–25). The antagonism may seem absolute,

but it will be resolved in favor of redemption: "In the world you face persecution. But take courage: I have conquered the world!" (16:33).

World Renewed

I have great respect for the Johannine view that the character defined as the world is an opponent in our quest for truth, light, and life. Biblically, the world has a poor track record in these elements, while harboring deceit, darkness, and death all along the way. But the world must not be confused with Mother Earth, the natural realm, our humanity, or your dog and houseplants, for that matter. The world that God made, loves, champions, and saves is not the enemy of God. Creation is a good thing, remember? Creation — you and me included — is beloved.

As dim as the Johannine portrayal of the world seems to be, it's the dark overlay of sin's shadow on creation that is the real villain of the piece. Creation itself is groaning for release, Paul tells us, as much as we are (Rom. 8:19–23). Christ is, after all, the firstborn of creation who holds it all together and seeks the reconciliation of heaven and earth (Col. 1:15–20). This home of ours is therefore not to be despised or sloughed off as irrelevant in the scheme of things. For what awaits us is "a new heavens and a new earth" that restores rather than repudiates the old one (2 Pet. 3:13; Rev. 21:1). Creation is not a failed experiment in God's eyes. It is a beauty hidden under the tarnish of history, and in the final defeat of evil, its brilliance will be revealed. World is going to get a second chance.

Read, Explore, Discuss

Genesis 2 and 3: Creation is subject to sin

Job 38–42: God speaks to Job

Ecclesiastes 1–6: The vanity of the world

Proverbs 8:22–36: Wisdom at the foundation of the world

Psalm 104: In praise for the goodness of creation

John 15–17: Choosing the world or Jesus

1 Corinthians 13: Attributes of the Divine

1 John 4: In the world but not of it

In the Spirit of Responsive Listening

- Reflect on the broken elements of your family history. How do you heal, or reinforce, this legacy?

- Consider the list of capital (deadly) sins: pride, envy, greed, anger, sloth, lust, and gluttony. Name the one that creates the most distance between you and God.

- The world suffers from acts of injustice, violence, and disunity. What do you do for justice, peace, and the spirit of community?

- List concrete steps you can take to avoid cynicism and despair about the present condition of the world.

STORY

NEXT TO ACTUALLY LIVING, telling stories is probably our most important activity. This is why Hollywood will never close down and novelists will never be out of work. People need stories, and someone will always figure out how to supply them. "Tell me a story" is one of the first refrains of childhood, and despite our advancing years, we never stop asking for more.

Our insatiable appetite for stories is a good thing. Stories tell us who we are and *why* we are. They present theories of meaning as varied as the genres in which they're told. Romance novels say life is about chasing down your one true love. Action movies tell us it's about discovering the hero within. Dystopian fantasies insist life is learning how to survive despite the system and the odds. Science fiction presents the pleasure and the peril of our love affair with technology. Buddy stories tell us the journey is the destination, so choose your companions wisely.

Storytelling seems to have been a human pastime since the invention of language. It can be casual, as when we call up a friend and ask, "How's it going?" Or it can be formal, plotted, and purposeful, like the writing of *Moby Dick*. Even the simplest narrative about our lives interprets what it all means and where the goals lie. Wherever the story is going, needless to say, it's taking us along for the ride.

Biblical stories employ many of the same forms we use to describe our own experience. Some utilize historical events, like the books of Chronicles, Maccabees, and Acts of the Apostles — admittedly with a generous layer of "spin" involved to guide the reader to the writer's intended conclusions. Other biblical works are purposeful fables, such as the tale of Balaam's ass in Numbers chapters 22–24, or the books of Jonah and Tobit. Some passages are theological reflections presented in mythological form: the creation story in Genesis and the book of Revelation come to mind. A little of everything can be found in Scripture: poetry and song, prayer and prophetic oracle, Wisdom proverb and moral instruction, letters and parables.

It would therefore be unfair to read the whole Bible from a single unyielding perspective. We would never demand that a modern song, novel, and news report all be understood as literally true, for example — even though each communicates something true within its own genre. The Bible is not purely a devotional work, though a book like Judith might be understood this way. The Song of Songs can be read as a sacred metaphor about Christ and the church, but it's also undeniably a love song celebrating sexual desire. We ought not to consider the predictions of Ezekiel and Daniel in the same light as a forecast about tomorrow's weather. Nor can we insist that everything told of Abraham, Isaac, and Jacob in the Genesis narratives transpired in history precisely that way.

When Scripture was written, "history" as a literary category hadn't been invented yet. As ancient people wrote about the past, they felt free and even obliged to embellish the stories to make their intended meaning more apparent. No one felt a responsibility for journalistic accuracy; the goal was to communicate the lessons of the past memorably. Nor would it have been possible to report "just the facts" even if someone had a mind to. Biblical stories were rarely written by eyewitnesses; mostly they were composed centuries after the generations they describe. There was no library of sources to consult, only communal memory and the imagination. Stories were punched up by the craft of the storyteller and tilted deliberately in the direction of their moral or intended instruction. To the ancients' way of thinking, this was not dishonest. This was the storyteller's job!

For those who read Scripture as salvation history, the word "history" may sound weighted toward a literal interpretation of its contents. To suggest that the Bible employs ahistorical elements can sound like an admission that it's "all made up" and therefore false. Rather, I'm strongly advocating that everything in the Bible is true. Even the stuff that never happened. Because the truth of storytelling trumps the truths of history for those who have an appreciation and respect for both. History is an account of the past. By definition, it's locked into the particulars of time, place, culture, and people. In a given context, then, historians strive to be accurate and impartial — but even they must interpret the facts they present. The best historians struggle to unlock the door of a particular past so that we can all learn from it in the present.

By contrast, pure story — the kind unmoored by actual historical events — takes place "once upon a time." It speaks of any generation, or every generation. Story presents what is universally, we might say even chronically, true. It seeks to reveal how *people* are, not how this group of people once was in their moment in time. The tools at the storyteller's disposal may include historical events and personalities, but the resource of invention is liberally utilized. To present truths higher than history, to reveal the truths of eternity, the storyteller is not bound simply to what was, but is attentive to what "is and was and is to come."

Consider how Jesus uses storytelling in his ministry: "A sower went out to sow." Who? When? Where? What? None of these questions are answered in the parable. A historian would be ashamed to turn in such a sloppy and inadequate report. What this parable means to tell us is *how* the sowing is done: generously, flamboyantly, almost giddily, giving every inch of soil an opportunity to be responsive. This is not an agricultural report from first-century Israel about shockingly careless farming methods. Rather, it's a revelation about how God offers the divine word to us. The interpretations of such a story are wide open, as is the experience of each new generation of listeners.

What's Past Is Prologue

It can't be stressed enough: the Bible is not primarily about the past, any more than your life is primarily about what's behind you. If we read Scripture as the ancient history of an exotic people in a faraway land, we effectively kill it. A living word has to breathe, and for believers, this word has the breath of God in it. A living word does say something about the past, for sure. But it also speaks of tomorrow and, more importantly, of today.

The story of your life serves as the best example of a living word. When you tell your story — however old you are or however long it is — the tale's not finished. All of what you say about your personal history is prologue to who you are now and what happens today. In fact, today's events may change how you view the past altogether. The nagging stepmother may become the hero of the piece if it turns out she was right. Being fired from that comfortable job may turn out to be the best thing that ever happened to you. We hold out hope for growth and conversion, even deathbed transformation, which can change the moral of the story at the eleventh hour. Even after death, according to Catholic teaching, the prayers of those who love us can shape and support our progress as our story in eternity continues to unfold.

Years ago, I met a very old priest who reminded me how essential it is not to lose hope in the promise of our own story. This man was an alcoholic. His years as a pastor were spent bouncing from one assignment to another as he drank his way through each. Finally he entered a rehab program to get sober, and when he returned, he had to face his bishop. At that meeting, the bishop told the aged priest regretfully that he could not give him another parish. Frankly, he was unassignable: across the diocese he had scandalized every parish he had served. The bishop had no place left to send him.

"Well, then," the priest replied, "assign me to that patch of ground the diocese owns outside of the city."

This request startled his superior. "But there's nothing out there," the bishop protested. "It's just stone and weeds!"

The old priest was resolved. "There's no one there to scandalize. I'll become a hermit and build a monastery out of that stone."

The bishop shook his head in dismay. "You're an old man, my friend; you won't live to see your monastery completed."

"I don't need to complete it," the priest replied. "I only need to build it."

I met the elderly priest when he was several years into his recovery. He was still building his monastery, stone by stone. From time to time he gave retreats to support himself and to share what he was learning out there in the silence. As far as I could tell, out of the ashes of this man's humiliation, God was building a saint.

Who was this man, really? The idealistic young person who first entered seminary, or the notorious drunk known to later parishioners? Was he the chastened man who went trembling into rehab? Or the humble priest who emerged, seeking a way to pick up the pieces of his shattered vocation and to allow God to make use of him again? All the stages of the old priest's life are "true" and belong in his story. But it would be grossly untrue to pin him to any earlier stage and leave him there — just as it would be to say, of Mary Magdalene, that a woman who once had seven demons in her can never be trusted.

The Bible Is Our Story

We noted that the Bible is best understood not as the story of God, but as the story of God's people. This makes it our story as much as it belongs to Adam and Eve, Moses, Mary of Nazareth, and Paul. Rather than regarding Scripture as a forbiddingly foreign work, we should pick it up with as much curiosity as we would a photo album in our grandparents' attic. Here, we find portraits of familiar people we almost recognize. They have our hands, our eyes, that improbable bit of hair that sticks up no matter how we comb it. This relative was a carpenter, and we have an aptitude for woodworking too. That one had a penchant for mischief; we're famous for that same sense of humor. We share an identity with the people in the photos as deep as our DNA. Though they wear antique clothes, they are more like us than our peers. The same blood flows in their veins as in ours.

The Bible is the story of our spiritual aunts and uncles, cousins, and siblings in the faith. They may talk a little funny, depending on the translation we're using, but if we look closely at their portraits, we'll discover the resemblance. We are Jacob, making our way past life's obstacles with a few tricks up our sleeves. We are Ruth, gambling the future on a loyalty fiercer than the facts. We are Habakkuk, asking hard questions and expecting a frank response. We are Peter, talking tough over dinner but overwhelmed by the instinct for self-preservation in the critical hour.

Why enlist the stories of the Bible in our quest for self-understanding? Because the world, that ever-present character in our story, also attempts to tell us who we are. In the world-view of capitalism we are consumers, born to buy. Biology insists we're animals in the great chain of being, meant to score high in the procreative game. We are combatants in the survival of the fittest, say the pragmatists, obliged to stockpile power and wealth. Or we're random accidents in the universe, a mere "tale told by an idiot, full of sound and fury, signifying nothing," as two Williams, Shakespeare and Faulkner, phrased it.

Organized religions are also in the identity business, quick to define us as safe or foul according to their standards. Colonial-era preacher Jonathan Edwards famously described the human race as "sinners in the hands of an angry God." The Bible calls us sinners, it's true, but it has other names to chose among: children of perdition, yes, but also children of the light. Lost, certainly, but also found and carried home in loving arms. One of the most telling identifications is in the biblical idea that we are pilgrims on a journey through wilderness to a promised homeland. This search for belonging and home is a pretty good summary of what the mortal sojourn, and the Bible, is about.

How the Story Got Started

I give a talk in parishes with the improbable title: "The Old Testament in Ninety Minutes." It sounds like a comedy routine, the joke being that you simply can't cover the complexity and scope of the forty-six wide-ranging books of the Hebrew story in an hour and a half. This whirlwind tour of events, characters, and ideas at least offers a sense of the landscape of the Hebrew Scriptures. Scholars, no doubt, would be horrified by the liberties taken to reduce salvation history to sound bites. But biblical sound bites are better than no bites at all, and many folks remain sadly unexposed to these essential stories.

The rabbis have boiled down biblical history to four efficient words: "We sin. God saves." This remains the most useful summary, and might be featured on the cover of the Bible as a synopsis. However, capturing Scripture in four words brings to mind the Woody Allen line: "I took a speed reading course and read *War and Peace* in twenty minutes. It involves Russia." While it's true that biblical history comes down to human sinfulness countered at every turn by God's saving activity, knowing that is a poor substitute for savoring the story. "$E=MC^2$" may be an elegant description of the universe, but give me a starry night and a decent telescope and I'll appreciate "universe" more.

What follows here is a brief summary of how the Bible came to be and what it's about. This is not a linear retelling of the story from front to back. Instead, this is how scholars presently understand the motivations of those who wrote and collected these stories. So let's tune in to the time before the Bible existed for a few moments to get a sense of why it seemed necessary to create a definitive Hebrew holy book. Our story begins in what we properly think of as the middle of the Bible: the exile of the people of Israel to Babylon.

Something really bad happened in the sixth century B.C.E. A nation that claimed "in God we trust" had its faith shaken.

All the things the people had counted on — their country, their king, and the practice of their religion — were lost overnight. What had gone wrong?

Outwardly, the problem was obvious. It was the old story of war and conquest. No one needs a slide rule to understand why strong nations prey on weak ones. Centuries earlier, a similar event had occurred: the Assyrian empire had swept through the northern kingdom of Israel and destroyed it. Now the new empire of Babylon had marched in and seized the southern kingdom of Judah, crushing Jerusalem, looting its Temple, and dragging its king off in chains. The most useful citizens were shuffled off to Babylon. That much was plain. But why had God allowed these things to happen?

The deep thinkers of Judah-in-exile contemplated their national story to try to figure it out. They weren't interested in history, but in understanding. They didn't seek to retrace the past but to interpret the overall direction of its footprints. They had texts to guide them in their quest: prophetic writings, plus a rudimentary document of the law of Moses. They also had oral tradition, which is a lot more than just hearsay. Our twenty-first-century generation has in its collective memory a mostly fuzzy sense of the national past. By contrast, ancient oral tradition provided a fairly standard way of telling the national story. The truth seekers in exile had all of these elements at their disposal with which to come to grips with their present situation.

They also had problems to solve, as immediate as they were poignant. Their children, growing up in a foreign land, were attracted to the stories of other gods and the allure of foreign ways. In the streets of Babylon they absorbed a national identity not their own and a worldview highly discordant with the way the people of Abraham viewed reality. How to lure the children back to their true identity within the community of the God of Moses? It was to preserve the future, and not the past, that the work we now know as the Bible began to take shape.

Promises, Promises

Most of us reach a point, sooner or later, where we feel "the young people" are missing something vital in their sense of the world. We want the next generation to appreciate the values that make us who we are. We don't want them to take for granted the good things we gained for them nor to lose sight of the important work yet to be done. Our legacy to them may include money and infrastructure, but we dearly wish to leave behind more. What we want to communicate, as our lasting gift, is the story that has inspired us.

Israel's most precious story is a fabric woven of many promises between God and the nation. The saga properly begins with Abraham, although he doesn't appear until the eleventh chapter of Genesis. The preliminary material can be understood as proto-history, outlining the broader issues of God and the world and why the Creator of everything decides to gamble so much on Abraham to begin with. After hope for the world disintegrates in a disappointing spiral of events, God talks one man into an amazing proposition. How about founding a nation with a singular destiny: to be a conduit of blessing for every nation on earth? (Gen. 12:2–3).

The man, hereafter known as the father of nations, enters into the bargain. Abraham will receive heirs and land, pretty good news for an elderly fellow without either. What God gets in return is a new avenue through which to dispense the divine blessing. This, apparently, is all God ever wants: another opportunity to promote the world's original potential for goodness. Through Abraham's lineage comes a nation called Israel after his grandchild, Jacob — renamed after wrestling with an angel (Gen. 32:23–33). Interestingly, Israel means Contender. The Lord seeks a dialogue partner, but God always winds up having to wrestle one down before the conversation can begin. Isn't that how you and I wound up in this story?

Imagine the self-understanding of a people destined to dispense the divine blessing for the sake of the world! Obviously, ancient Israel had no sense of global reality, but even to impart blessing to its neighbors in the little world of the Near East is a most generous mission. What if a nation rose up today with a goal, say, to make the world a better place? Not by imposing its will or its ways, mind you, but by providing the means for God's blessings to flow through it to all — to be the deliberate conduit for "the universal destination of goods" as the Catechism teaches it (see *Catechism of the Catholic Church*, nos. 2401–49). What an astonishing national dream Israel had!

In Jacob's generation, however, the story takes an unexpected detour. Famine brings the children of Israel to Egypt, but slavery keeps them there until God supplies a deliverer in Moses. As Moses leads the now-sprawling nation out of bondage, he hopes to surrender it to God on the other side of the Red Sea and retire from service. Instead, he is commissioned to guide these people for the rest of his life. Abraham was promised a nation; Moses is the fellow who actually gets one. By all accounts, Abraham got the better deal. Moses' reluctant stewardship, recounted from Exodus through Deuteronomy, becomes the centerpiece of the Hebrew story.

With Moses, God makes more promises. Along with the previous pledges of nation (in tow) and land (up ahead), God promises to live with the people and to journey with them wherever they go. Many ancient civilizations believed their gods inhabited the land, sea, and sky around them. But whoever heard of a traveling God? Since when did divinity take up residence within a people? Such intimacy was unthinkable. What's more, God's decision to live inside the nation — literally to pitch a tent in its midst — would require the transformation of Israel. Immanent contact with the divine presence would be fatal for those unprepared to receive it. The people would have to become holy, as God is holy, to endure the proximity.

So Israel gets a law, to fashion the people in the ways of their God; and a Tent of Meeting, where God is concealed; and an Ark of the Covenant, upon which God's glory rests like a king on a throne; and a priesthood, to supervise the tending of holy things. The whole people will be "a priestly kingdom and a holy nation" (Exod. 19:6). Routine sacrificial offerings would help reinforce or reclaim this necessary state of purity.

It goes without saying that Israel fails miserably at being a holy people. Try as they might to stay pure (and honestly, they don't always try so very hard), they lapse into decidedly unholy behavior at the drop of a yarmulke. Proximity to God proves difficult to manage, demanding twenty-four-hour vigilance to remain "clean" as a conduit of blessing. God had promised Noah long ago not to wash the world clean in a literal way ever again. So instead of wiping out this latest disappointing generation, God simply waits them out. It takes the Egyptian generation forty years to die off, one by one, including Moses. Then Joshua, the new leader, takes the renewed community into the land of promise.

What if you were invited to become God's special dwelling place? What if the personal cost to you was to make of your life a spiritual temple worthy to house the Divine? What adjustments would you have to make to your present lifestyle to become that sort of living, breathing tabernacle? How is this commission different from, or the same as, the one you renew every time you receive the sacrament of the Eucharist?

Who's in Charge?

Moses had hoped God would lead Israel by direct decree once the people were delivered from Egypt. Maybe that was even a possibility before the hour at Sinai when the nation, invited to encounter its true Deliverer in the great theophany, backed away and begged Moses to serve as go-between (Exod.

19:16–25; 20:18–21). This decision to deal with the Lord only through an appointed representative has indelible ramifications, as biblical decisions often do. Ever after, somebody has to take charge of the nation and to serve as ambassador of the divine will. Someone, like Moses, has to be strong enough to stand in the breech between God and Israel.

Being God's ambassador is no mean feat. Anyone wearing the uniform of clergy or religious personnel today knows the sobering responsibility that goes along with being one "who comes in the name of the Lord." Even if you and I don't wear so much as a cross or a medal, our baptism marks us as God's people, and we are the face of Christianity in everything we say or do. For those who look to our example, we speak for God. We can therefore sympathize with those in the biblical story drafted to fulfill this role.

The priesthood of Israel will provide ritual mediation between God and nation in the Promised Land, as they did in the desert. But biblical priests do not serve as national advisors since that fateful hour when Aaron, the first high priest and Moses' brother, made a bad judgment call in the Golden Calf incident (Exod. 32:1–35). In Moses' time, judges appointed from among the elders of the community arbitrate the divine law. After the time of Joshua, judges continue to serve the community and famous ones — like Deborah, Gideon, Jephthah, Samson, and Samuel — do a sometimes brilliant, sometimes dreadful job of it.

Samuel is among the best judges, yet he is also the last. His generation demands the appointment of a king to unite and rule over them. After much resistance and some divine consultation, Samuel submits to this request. The first king, Saul, seems appointed merely to illustrate that a king is a bad idea. David is anointed next, garnering another divine promise: to establish the house of David forever. It's a strange pledge, considering that the kingdom united under David is divided by civil war after the reign of his son, Solomon. Historically, Israel will never regain territorial integrity, but will remain two kingdoms — northern Israel and southern Judah — until the kingdom to the north vanishes for good.

It would be historically suspect to draw a one-to-one correspondence between the priests of Israel and modern clergy, tribal judges and present juridical and military systems, or ancient monarchies and modern governments. What Israel's story actually offers is a means to evaluate leadership, authority, and power altogether. Who's in charge, and who gets to speak for God? What do those in positions of authority do with the advantages at their disposal? To whom should we listen, and with what criteria do we choose and assess our leaders? Do bad leaders invariably bring down the whole community with them when they fall? As we listen to the stories of Israel's many leadership models through the books of Joshua, Judges, Samuel, Kings, and Chronicles, we are invited to consider how we too wield power: in our homes and friendships, on the job, in the neighborhood, at the parish, in economic decisions and political alliances. It's easy to blame the Israelites for their many poor choices; it's harder to recognize how our own relationship to power is often quite broken and in need of attention.

One more divine promise completes the picture before Judah descends into exile. Not long after David becomes king, he frets about living in a fine palace when God dwells in a tent. When the nation was wandering, the tent made perfect sense; in these settled times, it is decidedly quaint. A mobile God can hardly serve the interests of a landed king. David decides that God should stay put, now that Israel isn't going anywhere. This decision must have sounded chilling to the writers of this story, exiled in Babylon.

David determines to build God a worthier home, which is how the Jerusalem Temple comes into being. Although God jests with David that the Lord of the Universe hardly needs to reside between walls like an earthly king, by the time of Solomon, the Temple is a done deal. God deigns to dwell in its Holy of Holies. But one day the prophet Ezekiel, writing in Babylon, will have a "flashback" vision of the hour that the glory of God departed both the Temple and Jerusalem, signaling the hour of imminent destruction (Ezek. 10:1–23).

What does it mean for us to "plant" the omnipresent God in predetermined places? Sacred spaces like shrine and chapel, while very helpful to finite creatures seeking a divine encounter, must not be confused with the confinement of Infinite Being. Yet how often do we see folks tripping over themselves in church so as not to allow their backs to be turned to the Tabernacle for an instant, for fear of being disrespectful — only to step outside the church and promptly start swearing, as if God were now out of earshot? To identify God too narrowly with holy times and places is to close our eyes to the constant reality of the Holy Presence. God remains mobile, with or without a linen tent.

Here we reach the end of an era in Israel's story. It was a time of promises in which the nation understood itself in relationship to the God of a particular people, land, king, and Temple. When Babylon breaches the gates of Jerusalem, this event seems to reduce the divine covenants to ashes along with the city. No wonder the exiles are stunned by this catastrophe. Babylon not only devastated their way of life, but also discredited the God they thought they knew. It would take the creation of the Bible, a retelling of the whole story from top to bottom, to help them find their footing again.

Gathering Up the Story

The final writers and compilers of the Hebrew story didn't pull an all-nighter to get the documents we know as the Old Testament together. It took generations, many authors, and not a few editors to sift through and organize the accumulated stories. Several versions of a story often existed in parallel traditions: these were included side-by-side rather than harmonized. The overall saga is by no means linear; comprehensive and contradictory is valued over streamlined and cohesive. Conflicting stories serve as ballast for the truths expounded in each — not to mention the weaknesses doubtless found in either version.

The holy books are still a work in progress after a generation passes in exile. Suddenly the Babylonian captives are liberated by the next conqueror, Cyrus the Persian. By now only a remnant of the community remembers Jerusalem first-hand and values that citizenship. These return home to raise up their civilization from ruins. After the exile, six more prophetic books are gradually added to the nine already circulating. The Pentateuch assumes its final form, along with the miscellany known simply as Writings. Among the Writings, the Wisdom books were the last to be added. Works like Sirach and Wisdom were probably completed a century before the time later known as the Common Era.

> *To identify God too narrowly with holy times and places is to close our eyes to the constant reality of the Holy Presence. God remains mobile, with or without a linen tent.*

It's not clear precisely when the covers of the Jewish Bible were closed, so to speak, to further input. All through the century that produced Christianity, rabbinical leaders argued the merits of Jewish texts composed in Hebrew and in Greek, produced within and outside of Israel. Around 100 C.E., the matter was settled for Greek-speaking Jews by an Alexandrian compilation known as the Septuagint. Hebrew-speaking Jews preferred a somewhat smaller canon, excluding those works composed in Greek. In the fourth century C.E., when Christians assembled their own Bible, they adopted the longer Septuagint version of the Jewish Bible for their first Testament. In the time of the Reformation, Martin Luther and others stood down from that decision and chose the shorter Jewish canon. As a result, Catholic and Protestant Bibles are unmatched in their content. Meanwhile, the Orthodox tradition, using still another early version of the Jewish Bible, has several additional texts unfamiliar to Roman Catholics.

If we continued the story of how the Christian Scriptures of the Bible came to be, it would sound like this: Something horrible happened in the first century C.E. The Temple in Jerusalem was destroyed — again. A community of faith had seen its leaders dragged off and martyred. What they had counted on — that Christ their King would come again expediently in glory — hadn't happened. They were barred from the practice of their religion and forced to flee Jerusalem. What had gone wrong? And what now?

If this sounds like a rerun of the crisis that led to the creation of the Hebrew Scriptures, then you are paying attention. The Christian community, newly exiled outside the gates of orthodox Jewish thought, began sifting through its texts and its history, seeking understanding. Scattered letters of Paul, sayings of Jesus written by Matthew, a curious new book called the Gospel of Mark, and the stories already shaped into oral tradition were floating around Asia Minor. Time to gather, formulate, add, and edit. A new generation would contribute its genius to the story of salvation history.

Nineteen centuries after the biblical story has officially been closed, the story of salvation continues to unfold. I'm reminded of a priest I once met with a remarkable tattoo on the back of his hand. On closer inspection, I realized the image was a skull and crossbones. Printed underneath this insignia was a single word: "MAFIA." I asked him if his youthful indiscretions had caught up to him when he decided to be ordained. "I bet you never thought about giving out communion with that hand when you got that tattoo," I teased.

He laughed and admitted that he was only a teenager when that mark came into his life. At that time, his greatest desire was to join a gang known by the more-bark-than-bite moniker "Mafia." Part of the initiation rite involved tattooing your own hand with the gang name and sign. The very painful procedure had seemed worth it for the sake of belonging to the group.

And then the priest told me, "The strange thing is, five members of the original 'Mafia' gang went on to be ordained. And eight more became policemen. We may have seemed marked for trouble in the beginning, but God earmarked us for other purposes in the end." Just one more reason never to give up on a story that isn't finished. The last word on salvation, and on you and me, has yet to be written.

Read, Explore, Discuss

Genesis 12:1–9 and 15:1–15: Covenant with Abraham

Genesis 32:23–33: Jacob and the angel

Exodus 19 and 20: Covenant with Moses

Exodus 40: God has a dwelling place in Israel

1 Samuel 7: Covenant with David

1 Kings 6:11–13; 8:1–21; 9:1–9: Solomon and the Temple

Ezekiel 10:1–23: God's glory departs the Temple

Jeremiah 52:1–30: The destruction of Jerusalem

In the Spirit of Responsive Listening

◆ Reflect on promises spoken into your life: those made to you and those you have made. Resolve to be a better promise keeper.

◆ Evaluate how you tell your life story: Is it predominantly good news or bad? Who gets blamed and who exonerated? Is it a story of cynicism or hope?

◆ Over whom do you exercise authority? Pray for the grace to use power wisely.

◆ How portable is your God? Consider where and how you encounter the divine presence. Expand the territory.

Chapter Four —————————————————————

CRISIS

N O SANE PERSON seeks out the time of crisis. Most of us are creatures of comfort and stability. We prefer the familiar companion to the stranger, and the slow learning curve to sudden, dramatic events. If we could avoid change altogether, some of us probably would. Imagine a world with no nostalgia because "the good old days" never ended! A traditional Chinese curse reads: "May you live in a time of transition." If the worst thing we can wish on an enemy is transition, then surely events that spawn change are unlovable.

Crisis engenders the moment of decision. In the critical hour, action must be taken. Heroes rise to the occasion, whereas victims are crushed by it. Often we learn who we really are, underneath the pretense of roles we normally play, by what's called out of us in the hour of crisis.

My friend Dale, an admirable man during the years of our acquaintance, became even more luminous when he entered his last season of crisis. At sixty, Dale was a poster boy for physical fitness: a marathon runner, vigorous hiker, and rake thin. So I was stunned on the day I got word that he was in the hospital, facing death. He was paralyzed by a brain tumor, and for some weeks it was unclear whether or not Dale had the capacity to comprehend his condition. Even when he regained some speech, he didn't ask questions about his situation, as if such considerations were beyond him.

And then one evening, as I sat at his bedside, Dale asked suddenly, "Am I going to die?"

I had seen the medical reports. There was only one answer I could give: "Yes." Not an easy thing to say to someone you love. I took Dale's hand. For a moment we cried together. Then all at once his anger flared.

"I have things to do!" he shouted. "I need twenty more years!"

"You may only have *one* more," I said softly. "What do you want to do with it?" The idea left him speechless.

Death is the ultimate human crisis. In clinical terms, theologians describe death as a limit experience: on that evening, Dale could feel the edges of his mortality closing in. All limit experiences instigate crisis, whether the imposed boundaries involve disability or illness, ignorance or weakness or want. Eventually, we all bang against walls beyond which we can go no farther. Each limit experience is a painful and frustrating reality that we must nonetheless accept. The thing we want we cannot have. We cannot turn back the clock or change the rules of the universe to get it. We have to reconcile ourselves to human limitation. We may do this well or badly. Sometimes we opt for denial, but that serves us poorly when the facts are unavoidable.

Overnight, Dale had become physically disabled, and his thought and speech were belabored. Meanwhile the cancer was gaining ground. That was an awful lot to deny. However, losing twenty years from your life expectancy in the blink of an eye is a lot to absorb. I left him alone to give him some sacred space in which to stare down the dragon.

Within an hour, Dale called me back to his bedside. I was surprised to find him smiling, as if some great battle had been fought and won. "Can we have herb spaghetti for dinner?" he asked.

Surprise notched up to amazement. Since he'd returned from the hospital, Dale had shown no interest in food. Friends brought meals, but he toyed with the food politely. Unfortunately, it was my night to cook; my culinary talents cannot be underestimated. I told him honestly, "I don't know how to make herb spaghetti."

"But I do," he said. This was the most astonishing thing of all: Dale wanted to cook! So I helped him up into his wheelchair and he rolled into the kitchen, barking orders for pots and pans and ingredients. And together we made a marvelous meal and set a lovely table. We even opened a bottle of ancient Russian wine. Dale was in high spirits, and we laughed and talked like old times, and for that whole evening I almost forgot how sick he was, how close to death. My friend had looked over the edge of the cliff, faced his fear, and found his courage. Dying was still up ahead somewhere — but on that night, there was only spaghetti.

For those attentive to the divine story, it should be no surprise that renewed courage was expressed that night in a meal. Eating is an affirmation of life. That's why Jesus offers himself as food. In every Eucharist, Jesus invites us to step away from death, however close to the precipice we are, and embrace the life that has no end.

That night, Dale was jubilant as he sank back into his bed. "Thank you for a wonderful day," he said to me — on the night I told him he was dying. It *was* a wonderful day, one of the best I've known. What made it so good was that we had shared the truth. Jesus said it would set us free, but we don't always believe that. We often choose to hide from truths that are painful. But you know, the truth won't kill us. In fact, truth is the only thing that won't kill us. Deceit does kill, and yet so often we cling to that instead. Soviet writer Aleksandr Solzhenitsyn, who spent a great part of his life as a prisoner in a communist labor camp, wrote of his years in exile: "The first step in personal liberation is non-participation in the lie." If we want to be free, we have to stop participating in the comfortable lie and embrace the way of truth — which often arrives on our doorstep by means of crisis.

Biblical Crisis

If everything were copasetic with the human race, we wouldn't need a Bible — or religion, for that matter. The religious impulse arises from the incongruity of a good world threaded with evil and suffering, tending toward death. The origin of sin, as the story goes, generates the first crisis. Humanity forfeits the untroubled environment of innocence to descend into a new reality of care and hardship — World 2.0, we might say — which is the "genesis" of choosing against God's will. Every occasion of sin thereafter spawns other crises, large and small, national and personal. Each one initiates its own hour of decision.

Sin is not the only predicating factor of crisis. Opportunities for growth and change likewise quicken the critical hour. When Israel is delivered from slavery in Egypt and invited to step into liberty, the crisis of that hour is marked by lamb's blood on doorposts and lintels. The doorway of blood is, metaphorically, the passageway to freedom (Exod. 12:21–27). We might doubt that anyone would hesitate between slavery and liberty. Choosing the road out of Egypt also entails trusting in a God they can't see and in Moses, a leader who speaks poorly and is only nominally one of them because of his peculiar personal history. Those reluctant to embrace the risk involved in change might well think twice about such a billed "opportunity."

Each new passage into freedom and hope brings yet another decision. "See, I have set before you today life and prosperity, death and adversity," Moses warns the people at the end of their forty-years' journey through the wilderness. "Choose life so that you and your descendents may live, loving the LORD your God, obeying him, and holding fast to him" (Deut. 30:15, 19–20). The blessing and the curse are laid before the people repeatedly as they near the land of promise. How often do they — and we — choose the way of death and call down its inevitable curse!

The deepest hour of crisis for Israel, of course, is the Babylonian exile of 587 B.C.E. Losing the land, monarchy, and Temple was shocking in its own right. But the enduring crisis is one of faith in the God of the promise. When the big three covenants appear to be revoked, is the Lord still their God? Equally disconcerting is the crisis of identity: In what sense can Israel regard itself any longer as the people of God?

At the eye of this storm lived the prophets. They navigated each roiling disaster of Israel's history lashed to their confidence in God. Let's be specific here and confine our concern to the classical writing prophets, those who committed their vision to posterity. Other prophetic figures existed in Israel's history. Patriarchs like Abraham were called prophets, as were Moses and his sister Miriam, and some judges like Deborah and Samuel. Also to be counted are the two most famous seers, Elijah and Elisha, known as the former prophets. These two were wonder-workers as well as divine message bearers. Contrast all these earlier characters with the writing prophets — three major and twelve minor — who pioneered a new form of leadership for Israel. Theirs was a subversive leadership, facing off against the visible power-mongers of their times: kings and queens, priests, and the wealthy class. Every generation from the eighth to the fourth century B.C.E. had its bevy of writing prophets. Each seer seemed to be in the thrall of the sixth-century disaster as if encircling the vortex of 587 B.C.E. in some mystical time warp. Some wrote to prevent or to warn of the great exile and others to denounce the culprits responsible. Some also crafted words of hope to be savored in exile and to be carried out of Babylon into the future restoration. Finally, their prophetic texts were edited and extended after the exile in the ongoing attempt to make sense of this unparalleled crisis.

Understanding the Work of Prophecy

The popular notion of prophecy is that it foretells the future. As we've noted before, the most important hour for the biblical writer (and reader) is the present. Prophets, like everyone else who writes things down, obviously have an eye on the future. But their proclamations have an immediacy and urgency that are intended for today — for every "today," including the one they inhabited.

> *At the eye of this storm lived the prophets. They navigated each roiling disaster of Israel's history lashed to their confidence in God.*

So while we can legitimately read the Emmanuel prophecies of Isaiah in light of the Christian story to come — "For a child has been born for us, a son given to us" (Isa. 9:6) and other familiar readings of the Advent season — we should also acknowledge that these words had a parochial meaning for Isaiah's generation: the birth of the present king's son and the hope of his reign. Likewise, within the description of the suffering servant of Isaiah — "like a lamb that is led to the slaughter . . . so he did not open his mouth" (Isa. 53:7) — is undoubtedly an image in which Jesus recognized himself and his mission. At the same time, we must admit that Isaiah likely saw his own life of prophetic witness, and perhaps even the fate of Israel altogether, in those terms.

Far from making prophecy less useful, the relentless immediacy of these proclamations reminds us of the "living" dimension of Scripture. God's breath is in each declaration, so these words were not simply for the prophet's generation or the first century of Christianity (although clearly speaking to both); they also have something true and vital to communicate in our generation too, and into our individual lives. What hope is being born into our time — and into your life and mine? To what kind of suffering are we subject, and will we be as faithful in ours as Isaiah's servant was in his?

Isaiah is the major contributor of the first wave of writing prophets in the eighth century B.C.E. His "beat" was Jerusalem in the southern kingdom of Judah, as was that of his contemporary, Micah. Within the same century and probably writing even earlier were Amos and Hosea, both operating in the northern kingdom of Israel. The crises facing each kingdom were both separate and related. The north had a legitimacy problem that was easy to appreciate. After Solomon's kingdom erupted in civil war, southern Judah retained Jerusalem with its monarchy and Temple. While a smaller territory by far, having "God and king" on its side gave the south an aura of moral superiority. Meanwhile the northern kingdom, holding on to the name Israel and benefiting from the considerable wealth of the land, had only the ancient shrines like Bethel and Gilgal through which to continue the worship cult. The hilltop capital city of the north, Samaria, was agreeably defensible. It was also under scrutiny by hungry Assyria and marked for destruction.

Apparently it was Amos who jumpstarted the prophetic enterprise of the eighth century. A shepherd and orchardist of Judah, Amos is reluctantly compelled northward to warn his estranged cousin Israel of impending danger. Amos blames the injustice of northern society and the indifference of the rich for the Assyrian lion threatening to pounce. As an outsider, Amos gets no serious hearing. His local northern colleague, Hosea, takes up the prophetic task but attributes the trouble to a different source: the nation's infidelity and its illegitimate shrines and government. Both prophets have a point, but neither one is heeded. The northern kingdom falls to Assyria and is wiped from history for good.

Meanwhile Micah and Isaiah warn the citizens of Judah that they are also in danger since many of the same charges could be leveled against them. Perhaps because of their eloquent intervention, the south is spared — but only for the moment.

Injustice and infidelity are the twin devils that confront the people of God in the time of classical prophecy — and in every age. Jesus will one day link them together in his teaching: "Truly I tell you, just as you did it to one of the least of these who are members of my family, you did it to me" (Matt. 25:40).

The Prophets' Lunchroom

After Assyria destroys the north, one might hope for a respite in regional disaster. History rarely works this way. One good crisis often leads to another. The often grim eighth-century prophets hand the baton to the anxiety-driven seventh-century lineup of Zephaniah, Nahum, Habakkuk, and Jeremiah. These are prophets of Judah, of course; there is no more Israel per se. While it's easy to imagine that these four fellows, walking the same streets of a tiny kingdom, must have enjoyed hours of discussion and debate in some prophets' lunchroom in Jerusalem, this would be an oversimplification. While earlier prophets did influence the content and style of those that came later, seers were sufficiently spread across each century so as to have enjoyed little if any actual camaraderie.

Isaiah, for example, quotes Micah in his well-remembered line about beating swords into plowshares — or did Micah, of the same generation, quote Isaiah? (Compare Mic. 4:3 to Isa. 2:4.) These two men were compatriots of Jerusalem and may have known each other. Four centuries later, however, the prophet Joel takes up these same words and painfully twists them backwards in his post-exilic and pessimistic vision of apocalyptic war (Joel 4:10). Clearly prophets were attentive to each other, viewing recorded prophecy just as we do today, with an eye to its usefulness and applicability for the generation at hand.

Jeremiah, the major prophet of the last pre-exilic generation, gives us the most prolonged look into the life of a seer. We share the world Jeremiah inhabits through his passionate, personal style. As "autobiographical" as he seems, Jeremiah was also an aggressive reader of the prophets of the previous two centuries and incorporates their themes seamlessly into his work. Consider Jeremiah's use of Zephaniah's best contributions to the prophetic canon. Zephaniah picked up Amos's offhand reference to a day when the Lord's justice would be redressed and turned it into a profound metaphor: the apocalyptic and decisive Day of the Lord! Jeremiah exploits this new doomsday icon, as well as Zephaniah's choice phrase, "the faithful remnant." The remnant becomes a biblically resounding metaphor for all who stick with God through the crisis of history and are delivered safely to the other side of it. The remnant may emerge at the end of the present jeopardy, or ultimately, as in the book of Revelation.

Unhappily for Jeremiah — yet fortunately for us — he is the prophet who accompanies the citizens of Jerusalem through the cataclysm of 587 B.C.E., when city, nation, monarchy, and Temple are shattered. Jeremiah is kidnapped by his own fleeing countrymen and dragged off to Egypt, where tradition tells us he was eventually murdered. Through this season of national and personal disaster, Jeremiah provides us with front-row seats. He also gives us such a moving example of how to behave and believe in the critical hour that he becomes, for Christians, a foreshadowing of Jesus.

Prophecy in the Midst of Crisis and Beyond

Prophecy might seem most useful when it comes *before* a crisis. At this stage, it cautions us to change our course, possibly averting disaster. Prophecy also has its uses within the period of crisis. Just as an early warning in prosperous times unmasks the false security of that hour, so a word of hope whispered into the season of despair can remind the people of God that this, too, is not the last word on the subject of us.

Two prophets wrote during the Babylonian period: Ezekiel and an admirer of Isaiah's ideas known as Deutero-Isaiah. The eighth-century Isaiah was responsible for chapters 1–39 in the current text we have by that name. Chapters 40–55, however, reflect the hand of someone immersed in the Babylonian situation and trying to make sense of this wrenching period. This "second Isaiah's" vision of how faithful suffering is lifted up into glory according to God's design raised the hopes of his generation — and would become the blueprint for understanding the way of the cross for the Gospel writers. Contrast these writings with Ezekiel's message, written in the same generation but in the apocalyptic style: cerebral, mystical, and otherworldly. Deutero-Isaiah speaks from within human experience, and Ezekiel offers a celestial perspective on the crisis. Both anticipate a glorious restoration for the nation.

Listening to the prophets of the pre-exilic and exilic times, we grasp how prophecy speaks in advance of crisis, with words of warning and correction, as well as from within the maelstrom of disaster, with encouragement and hope. But what does it have to say after the fact, in the bitter and sometimes depressing season of restoration when the task ahead seems insurmountable?

Enter the final biblical writing prophets: Haggai, Zechariah, Malachi, Joel, Obadiah, and Jonah. (Some scholars add Trito-Isaiah — a third writer of the popular Isaiah "school" responsible for chapters 56–66 of that book.) It must be admitted, these guys get the most thankless job in prophecy. Some of us might covet the moral high ground of the pre-exilic prophet, zealously pointing out the sins of our generation.

Or we may be attracted to the beloved posture of the exilic prophet, Comforter-in-Chief for a grieving nation. But the post-exilic prophets get the job of reinventing the nation while staggering across the ruins of the old one. Returning to Jerusalem with the remnant generation, the temptation to mutter I-told-you-so must have been strong. It would also have been enormously unhelpful. Instead, Haggai and Zechariah employ their vision in the direction of restoring the monarchy and the Temple. As students of the school of Ezekiel, they are convinced that glory will return to the nation once these two central institutions have been reinstalled. Alas, prophecy alone cannot turn the tide of politics. The new Persian Empire that permitted Israel's return — a move deemed good for the empire, not necessarily for the exiles — is not going to tolerate rival kings within its reaches. The monarchy in Jerusalem will not be recovered, unless you count the puppet Herodian kings installed by the later Roman Empire. Most Jews would not. Hopes for a return of the house of David, at least in political terms, are eventually mothballed.

The Temple, however, will have its second period, rebuilt by the fifth century B.C.E. and gloriously refurbished in the time of the Herodians. Destroyed once more by the Romans in 70 C.E., the Temple too turns out to be a dead end for Israel's future.

Later books of prophecy seem disillusioned by the realities of history. Micah finds little to his liking in the restoration of Temple religion: the priesthood is as flawed as ever. He wagers his prophetic chips on the return of Elijah, the archetypal wonderworker of old. Meanwhile Obadiah broods on the bitter past, and Joel gets caught up in a destructively cleansing, apocalyptic future. Whoever wrote the satirical novella of Jonah seems to view the prophetic tradition altogether with a wry wink at its own inconsistencies and limitations.

When we sit in the assembly on Sundays and hear brief passages of prophecy proclaimed in church, most of us aren't mentally engaged in consigning these messages to their respective periods. We aren't concerned with an ancient people once poised on the brink of catastrophe, or falling into its maw, or climbing back out onto the ash heap of a barren-looking future. Understanding the original context of these passages may aid in appreciating some of their more alien features: the remarkable violence, the strongly worded condemnations, the glee at episodes we find quite grisly. On the other hand, knowing the context assists us in interpreting these passages for ourselves. How is our present culture close to the edge of a precipice from which it should be warned away? In what ways has our society already dropped into despair and how do these hopeful words console us? Have we learned yet that political solutions to spiritual problems don't work? How do we change not merely the exterior elements of a society but its interior composition?

Changing Lanes

Once I offered the Scripture reflection at a Mass for parochial school kids. The Gospel for the day was about Jesus telling his disciples to beware of religious leaders who take seats of honor in the assembly and act piously on street corners but do not practice what they preach. I asked the kids if they had ever played "Follow the Leader." Most raised their hands to indicate they knew the game. I asked them, "So what do you do when the leader climbs a tree?"

"You climb the tree!" they shouted.

"And what do you do when the leader runs real fast?"

"You run real fast!" they answered.

"And what do you do when the leader jumps up and down?"

"You jump up and down!" they said.

"And what do you do," I asked, "when the leader jumps off a cliff?"

Without missing a beat, those kids cried out with one voice, "You *don't* jump off the cliff!"

"That's exactly right," I affirmed. "You've obviously been well led by *your* parents and teachers. One of the lessons you learn from playing Follow the Leader is that sometimes you *don't* follow the leader — if that leader isn't wise, if he or she is leading you into danger. When the leader's not a good leader, you choose another one, or you go home and play something else. Because some leaders, Jesus tells us, are not wise or trustworthy." And some of them, as the children's lectionary delicately translates it, "Say one thing and do something else" (Matt. 23:3).

So I asked these schoolchildren if they knew the word for people who say one thing and do something else. "Hypocrites!" a boy shouted. Are we surprised that kids learn this word pretty early on? They live in a world run by adults, don't forget, so they know all about hypocrisy. About being told to eat their vegetables while the adults down junk food. About being told not to smoke and watching grownups light up all around them. About being sent to church when their folks stay behind at home. About being punished for swearing or talking back while adults model this behavior incessantly.

Hypocrisy thrives nowhere better than in the environment of religion. It's in this rich territory that good and evil are defined and their behaviors distinguished. How easy, then, to adopt religious behaviors, language, and positions, while harboring a very different spirit inside. No wonder that the realm of religion is subject to a unique kind of crisis. Spiritual crisis results when the superficial aspects of religiosity are exposed for what they are, and the cracks in the system are revealed to be deeper than they first appeared.

Throughout biblical history, two great religious ideas keep the people of God moving forward: law and prophecy. Religious law establishes the divinely approved boundaries of social behavior, and prophecy sounds the alarm when those boundaries are not honored. These two principles operate like kayak paddles, dipping into the water on either side of the boat as needed to propel the nation forward. Both rely on divine revelation for their authority. The law was handed down from heaven on a mountaintop. Prophecy is delivered by a celestial messenger like an angel, or through a voice heard, a vision seen, or a sign interpreted.

Precisely because law and prophecy rely on revelation, religion becomes a rather simple game for cheaters to play. Kings could point to their own divine appointment to back up their decrees — and even today, how many governments hide behind God for credibility! Pretenders of any rank can also fulfill the outward rituals of piety while two-timing morality in their faithless hearts. In the same way, false seers flourished through the era of the biblical prophets. These yes-men and yes-women were handsomely compensated for delivering the message most likely to please the court they served. In the final analysis, law and prophecy are only as good as the intentions of the people who claim these authorities. Divining God's will when those who speak for God are untrustworthy can be a daunting situation. Those of us who have been discouraged by our own leaders — in the arena of government or religion — will appreciate the magnitude of the challenge.

Enter the Wisdom Tradition

After the exile, when the future of monarchy, priesthood, and even prophecy seemed uncertain, a new authority captures the imagination and buoys the hopes of at least a portion of the people of God. How many would be hard to say; possibly the majority was never attracted, but certainly educated members of the community would have given it a hearing. It's important to note here that not all of "Israel" lived in Israel anymore. After the sixth century B.C.E., the greatest number of the children of Abraham lived abroad. This population became known as the *Diaspora,* or dispersed ones. Diaspora Jews were influenced by the cultures they inhabited: Babylonian, Persian, Egyptian, and eventually Greco-Roman. These societies enjoyed robust Wisdom traditions and so Judaism expanded its Wisdom teaching as well. Israel had such literature before this time: David wrote verse, and Solomon's reputation for wisdom attracted a far-off queen of Africa. But the Wisdom writings of Israel seem to flower after the resettlement of the land in the last centuries before the Common Era.

In the Bible, Wisdom literature is fairly easy to spot. Sometimes genre is the dead giveaway: proverbs, fables, and codes outlining household behavior are classic forms of Wisdom teaching. But Wisdom is better distinguished for its themes: its tireless distinctions drawn between righteousness and wickedness, as well as its preoccupation with the origins of evil and suffering. Some biblical books fit entirely into the Wisdom category — Proverbs, Wisdom, Sirach, Ecclesiastes, Job, and the Song of Songs. Some scholars also see the hand of Wisdom authors at work in the creation stories of Genesis, the fable of Balaam's ass in Numbers, certain psalms, and even the Letter of James and the household codes of Paul in the Christian era.

Wisdom writers are remarkably uninterested in the history of Israel. Only Sirach and the writer of the book called Wisdom even mention the past in any detail. This great omission may have been a feature of Diaspora writings or a deliberate attempt to avoid the quagmire of musing about that all-encompassing era of 587 B.C.E. Wisdom writers prefer to write on a wider scale: about humanity, not just the nation. They write about every feature of life, not merely religious rituals and principles. Most significantly, Wisdom writers ground their authority not in revealed truth but in the world around them. They aren't atheists; some are quite pious, and nearly all exhibit belief in a divine bottom line. Their reverence for the world has to do with their faith in the inspired order and meaning of creation. If God is the author of the world, so Wisdom teaching goes, then to know the mind of God, you must study the world.

We sense immediately the radical nature of this claim. In a sentence, religious authority is swept out of the hands of kings, priests, and prophets and delivered into the possession of — just about anyone. Wisdom teachers do insist that you do your homework: learning from the world isn't something accomplished in a glance or unsystematically. The Wisdom school depends more on faith than on religion: more on the designs of nature and the observable truths gleaned from people-watching than on ritual and creed. In this sense, Wisdom holds a more optimistic opinion of the human race than either law or prophecy does. Wisdom insists that people don't need to be commanded, forbidden, or frightened into doing the right thing. They can also be taught, through observation and the use of reason, to embrace how the world works and to surrender to the proper course of action.

If ever a theological system spawned a religious crisis, it was this one. The Jewish understanding of God, originally launched on nationalistic claims, suddenly got a universal window. A religion tightly tethered to law and ritual was given free rein to pursue new avenues.

Wisdom Gets a Name

When we think "Old Testament," we tend to recall the stories of the Pentateuch and the books of prophecy. There's a tendency to dismiss the rest: those books clumped together in the miscellaneous category of "Writings." But many of those writings, rooted in Wisdom teaching, have more to do with the advent of the Christian story than anything else in the history of Israel. Wisdom teaching changed the rules and expanded the nature of religious authority. It created a climate wherein the people of God might begin to think outside the established theological box.

R. Charles Hill points out in his excellent survey book, *Wisdom's Many Faces*, that when we speak of the biblical Wisdom tradition, we are describing the teaching of Jesus as well. Jesus proves himself capable of wielding a saying or two: "For where your treasure is, there also will your heart be" (Matt. 6:21). "Do to others whatever you would have them do to you" (Matt. 7:12). Jesus also feels free to repudiate old proverbs as needed: "An eye for an eye and a tooth for a tooth" (Exod. 21:24; Matt. 5:28) becomes "Offer no resistance to one who is evil" (Matt. 5:29).

The fable-makers of old had nothing on Jesus, who is a master of the parable form. He is also perfectly at home invoking the designs of the natural world to confirm his teachings: "Look at the birds of the air." "Consider the lilies of the field." "Every good tree bears good fruit" (see Matt. 6:26, 28; 7:17). Jesus likewise keenly observes how practical matters illuminate spiritual realities: "New wine is put into fresh wineskins." "Suppose one of you has only one sheep and it falls into a pit on the Sabbath; will you not lay hold of it and lift it out?" (Matt. 9:17; 12:11).

Like other Wisdom teachers, Jesus emanates an authority that does not come from any official capacity in which he

serves, but rather derives from the message itself. It is no wonder that later writers would make the connection between the
feminine Lady Wisdom and Jesus. The Divine Word in the
first chapter of John's Gospel reflects the incarnate Wisdom
of Proverbs 8 and Sirach 24. St. Paul seems very comfortable repudiating worldly wisdom while asserting in the same
breath that Christ is "the power of God and the wisdom of
God" (1 Cor. 1:24). Putting on the mind of Christ and em-
bracing the indwelling Holy Spirit will satisfy those who seek
the hidden wisdom "decreed before the ages" (2 Cor. 2:7).

The introduction of the indwelling Spirit, of course, in-
augurates the potential for religious crisis in every age since
the morning of the Christian Pentecost. The Spirit remains a
wild card in the realm of institutional religion. "Authorized"
spiritual authority is claimed by the brave and the few. Yet as
long as the Spirit imparts its gift of wisdom, blowing where it
wills, divinely inspired activity can break out just about anywhere. Which is reassuring, since the next crisis is no doubt
right around the corner.

Read, Explore, Discuss

Exodus 12: Passover in Egypt

Deuteronomy 30: The blessing and the curse

Zechariah 3:9–20: The faithful remnant

Isaiah 7:10–16; 9:1–6; 11:1–9: Emmanuel prophecies

Isaiah 42:1–9; 49:1–7; 50:4–11; 52:13–53:1: Servant songs

Malachi 3: The Day of the Lord

Ezekiel 37:1–14: Vision of the dry bones

Daniel 12: Secret revelation of the end of days

Matthew 5–7: Jesus, Wisdom teacher

Matthew 25:31–46: Justice and fidelity linked

1 Corinthians 1:18–2:16: Christ is the Wisdom of God

In the Spirit of Responsive Listening

• Consider the resources you've used to navigate the crises you have faced so far.

• Listen attentively for the modern prophets who speak a challenging word daily into the world.

• Resolve to read the books of Wisdom teachers, both ancient and contemporary. Visit your local Catholic bookstore for ideas.

• Pray for a fuller reception of the spiritual gifts: wisdom, understanding, knowledge, counsel, courage, reverence, and wonder and awe in the presence of the Lord.

Chapter Five

TIME

A CLERIC WAS SUMMONED to the deathbed of a cloistered nun. Arriving at her cell, the priest found the woman standing on her narrow bed, arms spread wide, palms pressed against the doorsills of her room prohibitively. Shrieking, the nun proclaimed, "I'm not leaving! I LOVE this place!"

Most of us sympathize with this woman's posture toward mortality. We too have come to love this world and are loath to leave it, no matter what our circumstances are. But that ever-present symbol of mortality, the clock, is ticking all around us. You may be wearing a watch and carrying a cell phone that notes the time. So does the clock on the wall, the microwave oven, the DVD player, and the computer. Reminders of the passage of the hours are inescapable, along with calendars recording the days, weeks, and months of your journey. Somewhere in your life, there may be a date planner that tyrannizes each fresh day with its carefully noted appointments and obligations. Time can be a merciless bully, and we often feel like its prisoners. But the only exit from the tyranny of hours is one we seldom want to contemplate. In the days of grandfather clocks, the pendulum was deliberately stilled when death visited a house. Stopping a clock, however, never halts the relentless forward motion through which we are all propelled. As the moments tick by, they draw us to the final hour when our lives will be required of us.

The story of the Bible is inevitably the saga of time. It begins when God separates day and night, and it ends in a cycle of cataclysmic events described in the book of Revelation. " 'I am the Alpha and the Omega,' says the Lord God, who is and who was and who is to come, the Almighty" (Rev. 1:8). God starts and finishes everything — ultimately. Yet divinity exists outside of time and its effects. To God, "one day is like a thousand years, and a thousand years are like one day" (2 Pet. 3:8). G. K. Chesterton noted that, spiritually speaking, sin is the root cause of aging and death in our kind. This brings Chesterton to a startling conclusion: "Our Father is younger than we." Young as in ageless. God does not bore or tire. God does not cease to delight in the same repetitive pleasures of sunrise and sunset. Like a child, God remains amazed, amused, enthusiastic, and hopeful in every hour of history. God sees the constant potential of each new moment of time as if it were the first one. If we want to step into divine reality, as Jesus instructed, we have to become like little children: open to the possibilities in everlasting life.

For mortals, boredom and weariness can snowball as we accumulate the disappointments of a lifetime. We get seventy or eighty years if we're strong enough, as Psalm 90 suggests. But in the first handful of those years, many of us have already settled for a very abbreviated list of expectations of what life offers and what we can accomplish. We sell ourselves and others — and time itself — far short.

Look Twice

Impatience is a byproduct of mortality. Even though we don't deliberate on our limited lifespan every moment of the day, we still regard time as a precious commodity. Anything that gets in our way or slows us down becomes the enemy because it is wasting our time — and we don't have a moment to lose.

Another result of our ensnarement in time is that we rely heavily on first impressions, snap judgments, and predetermined biases to navigate new situations. As a result, we see little and observe less about what's actually going on. The art of contemplation is practically foreign to us. Unless we actively practice it, chances are we won't see beyond the surface of things and will come instead to erroneous conclusions about God, the world, and ourselves on a regular basis.

Finding time for contemplation isn't hard; we just have to be creative about it. If you need to be in a lotus position at the base of a waterfall in the middle of a forest to meditate, well, then you'll find few opportunities to employ this skill. But whenever a small stretch of time opens up to you — stuck in a traffic jam, waiting in a doctor's office, sitting through a boring meeting — consider it a divine opportunity to contemplate. My rule of thumb: if I catch myself glancing at my watch, I probably have the time to meditate.

The communion lines on Sunday morning are a natural source of contemplation for those unsure how to foster this skill. I remember watching an old woman maneuver tentatively up the aisle toward the sanctuary. Each step was a risk she seemed willing to take on frail legs toward a precious goal. At her side was a much younger man, presumably her son, who seemed to be supporting her by the hand on her journey. If I had looked away just then, I might have misread their story. As they drew closer to me, however, I realized that the situation was not as I had perceived at first glance. The younger man, I could now see, was himself plodding along, his eyes downcast. It was apparent that he had some form of mental impairment. The old woman was in fact guiding *him* by the hand to the front of the communion line.

Observing the Sabbath denounces the tyranny of the clock and honors the Lord of time.

As I continued to follow their journey up the aisle, gradually I came to understand what I was really seeing. The truth was neither as I had imagined in my first nor in my second stage of understanding. The old woman was indeed fragile and needed support. The younger man was certainly vulnerable enough to require guidance. And so he was lending her his strength even as she shepherded him, and *both* approached the Table of the Lord with the help of the other. They accomplished in tandem what they might not have been able to do alone. Unfolding in front of me was a vision of the church: how we come to the meal together with all of our brokenness, lending each other the encouragement necessary to take the challenging journey forward.

It takes time to see things as they really are, not as we imagine them to be. This is one reason why liturgical time is a valuable tool in the arsenal of the faithful. It provides a break from clock time, with its hourly demands regarding mostly mundane matters, and invites us to look beyond to eternal considerations. The celebration of liturgical feasts and seasons comes early into the story of God's people. Originally, these celebrations are tied to the cycles of agriculture and provided an opportunity to look up from the planting and harvesting to the source of all life and abundance. In the era of lawgiving, the Lord communicates to Moses the importance of honoring the gift of time: "Speak to the people of Israel and say to them: These are the appointed festivals of the LORD that you shall proclaim as holy convocations, my appointed festivals" (Lev. 23:2).

Given priority of place among "holy convocations" is the Sabbath day, a commemoration of God's own rest after the work of creation. If God relaxes after labor, how much more do we need the respite from the struggle to produce and provide! Through the centuries, rabbis will continue to argue that the commandment regarding the Sabbath is the most vital of the whole Decalogue. Observing the Sabbath denounces the tyranny of the clock and honors the Lord of time. It takes the burden of time out of our hands, if only for a day, so that we might lift our gaze beyond it. Appreciating the centrality of Sabbath observance helps us to better understand why Jesus created a furor every time he acted on the seventh day. Needless to say, the Lord of the Sabbath (Matt. 12:8; John

5:17–19) understood the sacred character of time much better than his contemporaries, living as he did under constant
awareness of the "hour."

Knowing the proper time to act and to refrain from activity
is one way of putting on the mind of God, as the ancient
Hebrews understood. God alone knows the time for things to
occur: "then [the Lord] will give you the rain for your land in
its season, the early rain and the later rain" (Deut. 11:14). The
Lord also keeps for the nation "the weeks appointed for the
harvest" (Jer. 5:24). If that weren't enough, God reminds Job
in the famous soliloquy from the whirlwind of the multitude
of nature's details that are divinely monitored so that they
occur "in due season."

Telling time, we begin to understand, is quite a bit more
complicated than knowing which digits are currently blink-
ing on the clock. St. Paul has much to say on the subject of
discerning the hour:

> You know what time it is, how it is now the moment
> for you to wake from sleep. For salvation is nearer to us
> than when we became believers; the night is far gone, the
> day is near. Let us then lay aside the works of darkness
> and put on the armor of light; let us live honorably as in
> the day. (Rom. 13:11–13)

The very nature of time changes for those who believe as
Paul does. No longer are literal day and night the departure
points for determining the hour. In this remarkable new era,
the light of Christ is revealed to be everlasting day for people
of faith. Paul voices his dismay with those who do not grasp

how the texture of time is altered: "You are observing special days, and months, and seasons, and years. I am afraid that my work for you may have been wasted" (Gal. 4:10–11). The calendar determined by the cycles of planting and harvesting has been superseded by the era of grace. Clock time has given way to God's timelessness, with its long view on eternity.

Time Meets Eternity

One extravagant idea transformed religion as usual in the century before Christianity. It expanded the horizon of human destiny beyond mortality. Humanity was once deemed pitifully ephemeral according to the Hebrew perspective:

> You turn us back to dust,
> and say, "Turn back, you mortals."
> For a thousand years in your sight
> are like yesterday when it is past,
> or like a watch in the night.

> You sweep them away; they are like a dream,
> like grass that is renewed in the morning;
> in the morning it flourishes and is renewed;
> in the evening it fades and withers. (Ps. 90:3–6)

The concept of afterlife enters this picture like a fox raiding the metaphysical henhouse. Afterlife is a dimension of the religious worldview that Christians take for granted today. Yet for most of biblical history, afterlife was not part of the religious bargain. God set limits on mortality in order to contain the amount of evil people might do, capping the human lifespan at 120 years (Gen. 6:3). The tree of life, representing the source of immortality, was off limits to the descendants of Adam and Eve (Gen. 3:22–23). The ancient theologian considered post-mortal existence in terms of the vague, shadowy holding-tank of Sheol (Job 17:13–16; Ps. 88; Isa. 14:9–11; 26:14). One could not speak of after*life* in Sheol; life implies purpose, movement, and possibility.

Then came the Wisdom writers, who dared to suggest that Wisdom herself is a tree of life (Prov. 3:18). While wickedness leads inexorably to death, the just path leads to the preservation of life (Prov. 2:18–19; 4:13; 6:23; 12:28). While these statements don't necessarily imply life-after-death as we speak of it, they do lay the groundwork for positing such a notion. Add these assertions to apocalyptic images like Ezekiel's dry bones vision (Ezek. 37:1–14) and Daniel's secret revelation of the end-times — "Many of those who sleep in the dust of the earth shall awake, some to everlasting life" (Dan. 12:2) — and you begin to sense a seismic shift in speculation and expectation. This shift reaches its fullest Hebrew expression in the deteurocanonical works of Wisdom and 2 Maccabees. Here we learn that "the souls of the righteous are in the hand of God . . . their hope is full of immortality" (Wisd. 3:1, 4). The story of the seven brothers who resist an earthly king in favor of a greater One marks an apex of pre-Christian belief in the resurrection: "You dismiss us from this present life, but the King of the universe will raise us up to an everlasting renewal of life, because we have died for his laws" (2 Macc. 7:9).

Afterlife upset the applecart of the Hebrew religious world-view in many ways. It transformed the idea of divine justice, for one. No longer was God's justice confined to this lifetime; rather, wrongs could be redressed in a time yet to be. The notion that the just prosper and the wicked come to ruin in this world — so often contradicted by experience — might finally be discarded as unproven and inadequate. You could no longer judge the players by the weight of their purses or the sores on their flesh. Who was on the side of God and who working against the divine purposes became an interior matter. You could not guess, from the clean outer rim of a cup, whether or not corruption festered inside (Luke 11:39–44).

A man named John comes baptizing in this era of theological mayhem. Unlike the Pharisees, who championed the metaphysical concepts of afterlife, spirits, and angels while nonetheless focusing on exterior behaviors and practices, John insisted on a frank confession of interior fault and a converted heart. Preparing the way of the Lord required dying to the old self and rising up from the Jordan River cleansed and renewed. When Jesus comes on the scene, the season of preparation is already past: "The time is fulfilled," Jesus proclaims — to a generation not unlike ours with an inadequate sense of the hour. "The kingdom of God has come near" (Mark 1:15).

Telling Time in the Kingdom

Ancient Hebrew was a simple language. Although modern languages have a plethora of tenses with which to express actions in the past, present, and future, along with various conditional options, Hebrew communicated two main frames of time: actions that had been completed, and those yet to be. Either something had happened or it had not. Language about time was not particularly elastic.

The story of Christianity, however, is written almost entirely in Greek. The evangelists and epistle writers compose their Gospel proclamation in language that could bounce — and a good thing, too, since the truths professed by Christianity have a lot of bounce in them. The proclamation of the reign of God announces an arrival that is yet to be, is happening now, and would be fulfilled later. The kingdom is near, at hand, and within you, all at once. At the same time that the kingdom is present and active in Jesus himself (Mark 4:30–32), Jesus urges his disciples to pray for its coming daily (Matt. 6:10; Luke 11:2). Yet later, when pressed at his trial, Jesus admits that his kingdom is not of this world and surely not in evidence here (John 18:36).

Theologians do their best to cope with what we might call the quantum inconsistencies of the divine kingdom. Some, like C. H. Dodd, spoke of the elusive character of God's kingdom in terms of "realized eschatology." Eschatology refers to the last things: the end of the world, final judgment, and everlasting destiny. God's great justice, according to Dodd and others, is "realized" in the person of Jesus: his life and ministry and identity. In a sense, Dodd steals the thunder of afterlife by intimating that everything we hope for has already come to pass in Jesus.

Jesuit Karl Rahner suggested that anything you say about the end-times is also true of the present as it moves into the future. This sounds a little like realized eschatology, only it assigns the "realization" to our lifetime rather than that of Jesus. We enter into the kingdom, or deny ourselves access, with every decision we're presently making. In a sort of compromise position, Jürgen Moltmann in *Theology of Hope* envisioned kingdom reality as the future breaking into time — perhaps the most elastic configuration of all. So here are three choices to consider: the kingdom is already fulfilled in Jesus; the kingdom starts now and tends toward the future; the kingdom exists in the future but loops back into the present to meet us.

Even if you understand that in English, none of it could be said in ancient Hebrew. But you can speak of *zikkaron*, the Hebrew word for appropriating the past for the present by ritual remembrance. For example, the annual Passover celebration makes God's deliverance of the nation from slavery — a past event — real and vital for the present generation of Jews. A similar Greek word, *anamnesis*, describes what Catholics understand to be the action of our Eucharist: the body and blood of Christ is made present in our assembly once more. This is why Catholics are very careful not to describe the Eucharist as simply a memorial meal. We are not remembering the past in a common sense, but recovering the past for the present in a most dynamic way. The power of "sacred remembrance" brings the past forward — just as theologians are suggesting that "holy longing" for the reign of God brings the eternal kingdom into time to meet us.

Kingdom Now

After being subjected to this much theology, it's biblically appropriate to tell a story. Biblical stories are, after all, about incarnation: making the things of eternity tangible. Most of us suffer from the reverse phenomenon. Our world is so incredibly concrete that it's hard to see past it. It's especially hard to see beyond the physical realities that prejudice or intimidate us. But that could be the first step in developing eyes for the kingdom. Jesus saw past "tax collector" and "prostitute" to the man and the woman struggling behind these roles. Paul generalized Gospel attitudes to advocate a new way of seeing beyond the distinctions of male and female, Gentile and Jew, slave and liberated. Kingdom sight is something we are all blind to, until Jesus touches our eyes and enables us at last to see the truth.

Years ago I studied in Berkeley, a town that prides itself on its accessibility for those living with disability. The result of such accommodation is that you see a lot of active citizens in wheelchairs. If you come from a less hospitable environment where such a sight is rare, you might find yourself paradoxically staring and averting your eyes until you get used to it.

Yet after living there for a decade, one afternoon I saw a fellow who caused me to stare. From a full block away, this man's unique burden and struggle were obvious. He sat in a motorized chair, his body slight like a child's, hardly fifty pounds in his maturity. His limbs were twisted and contorted like a human pretzel. Even his face was out of his control, gripped by grimaces many times a minute.

I wondered what it would be like, not to be able to smile. I had never seen suffering so complete. The thought of meeting this man distressed me terribly. I didn't even want to risk the casual encounter of passing on the sidewalk. I decided to cross the street, which would have been simple enough to do. That way I would not have to see him up close, would not have to meet his eyes, would not have to share, even for an instant, his reality. I did not want to know more about such suffering than was visible from a distance.

Moral cowardice is not something I like to admit. So as the impulse to avoid this man engulfed me, I began to wrestle with it. He was not asking me for anything. All we owe to passersby is an acknowledgment of their humanity. Passing this man on the street would take but a moment. Could I not give a fellow human being one instant of respect?

I walked forward, my heart trembling. And as this stranger and I entered that delicate zone of closeness where people acknowledge each other, I looked into his eyes and managed a small greeting, a timid smile. It was then that the kingdom of God broke through. This stranger, in this tortured body, attempted to smile out of one corner of his mouth. A crooked little half grin zigzagged across his face like a dancing sun peeping out from behind a cloud. Warmth, joy, and delight spread across his features. He was transfigured before my eyes. Suddenly I recognized his humor, his twinkling eyes, his excruciating beauty as a fellow traveler in the world. Light poured out from him and over me and into the street until it covered the whole scene like a radiant blanket. It happened all in an instant, a quick smile and a greeting, but as he passed by and the sound of his motorized chair buzzed down the street behind me, I broke into tears. I nearly knelt on the sidewalk. O my God, it was Jesus — and I almost missed him.

If the kingdom does break into time, it comes about in this way: an invitation wide open for an instant — "come and see!" (John 1:39) — but we have to be ready for it. Eternity does not linger. If we cross to the other side of the street, we may miss it entirely and never know what was waiting for us. At the same time, we must understand — because it's a realm of paradox — the eternal kingdom *always* awaits us and is *always* nearer than we imagine. If we've been paying any attention to the kingdom stories Jesus tells, it's erupting in a most surprising form in every moment.

Another example: on the old Feast of Corpus Christi, a man wandered into an urban church in the middle of Mass. The fellow was clearly mentally unstable and refused to sit down, choosing to roam the aisles instead. City people are inured to such distractions. This particular disruption moved beyond the acceptable, however, as the man began echoing the words of the presider in low but mocking tones.

When the priest reached the Eucharistic Prayer on this special feast of Body and Blood, the man in the aisles started shrieking and cursing as if possessed. The assembly froze, and the priest tried to continue the prayer under this blasphemous assault. Finally the priest abandoned the words of the rite and offered a spontaneous and heartfelt prayer for the Spirit of peace.

Just then a small child at the end of a pew slipped away from her parents and approached the deranged man. She took his hand and, as the astonished congregation watched, led him to a seat and sat down with him. He grew quiet at once. When it was time to offer the sign of peace, first the child's parents, then others in the community approached the man and shook his hand. The man sat through the rest of the Mass, gently weeping, and did not disturb the assembly again.

How can this be? As part of that once-frozen assembly, I saw no way out of an increasingly uncomfortable situation without an escalation of violence: a group of strong men restraining the intruder and dragging him away. A five-year-old saw it differently, acting simply, sincerely, and without fear. In one sense, she shamed the hundreds of adults sitting in pious indignation all around her. Yet in another, more important way, she led us to awe and wonder and praise by her example. Kingdom comes when God's will is done — and not a moment sooner. If we want to experience this "on earth as it is in heaven," we have to step confidently into the divine will.

The Holiness of Now

"Immediately" is one of the evangelist Mark's favorite words. He uses it forty-two times in his Gospel, expressing an urgency about the good news of Jesus Christ that is unmistakable. If these things we profess are true, Mark says, then we must act on them at once. The fulfillment of time is embodied in the person of Jesus. What are we waiting for?

If "immediately" is too quick for you, how about "today"? This is Luke's preferred usage in both his Gospel and the Acts of the Apostles. "Today this scripture has been fulfilled in your hearing" (Luke 4:21). "To you is born this day in the city of David a Savior, who is the Messiah, the Lord" (2:11). "Today salvation has come to this house" (19:9). "Truly I tell you, today you will be with me in Paradise" (23:43). This relentless present tense is quite deliberate: Luke wants these words to leap off the page into the lives of his readers.

Matthew employs some of Mark's immediacy but is also a fan of "now." Jesus speaks to John the Baptist's perplexity with these soothing words: "Let it be so now" (Matt. 2:15). To the leaders of the Sanhedrin Jesus declares: "From now on you will see the Son of Man seated at the right hand of Power" (26:64). The abundant kingdom parables in Matthew's Gospel describe the eternal realm in terms that are comfortably close and familiar. Jesus is also content to settle for the proximity of "always," as in "And remember, I am with you always, to the end of the age" (28:20).

The Gospel of John, while bearing the same good news as the other three, generally prefers doing so in its own unique terms. Key Gospel words like "kingdom" are rarely used by this evangelist. John develops the same eschatological ideas using the language of "eternal life" and "the hour." Eternal life, to John, is not the same as afterlife. The eternal life Jesus promises begins at once and extends forward forever. More properly, eternal life always "is" and it is *we* who step forward into it. When Jesus uses his famous Johannine construction, "I AM," he not only identifies with the ever-living God known to Moses by the same name, but he also states a Mark-like immediacy about the gift of life he offers. "I am the bread of life" (John 6:35). "I am the light of the world"

(8:12). "Very truly I tell you, before Abraham was, I am" (8:58). "I am the good shepherd" (10:14). "I am the resurrection and the life" (11:25). "I am the way, and the truth, and the life" (14:6). "I am the true vine" (15:1).

Not only does Jesus claim an essential identity in God his Father, but he also graciously extends that intimacy to us: "On that day you will know that I am in my Father, and you in me, and I in you" (John 14:20). The precise coordinates of "that day" may be unknown to us, but in the ever-elastic terms of the kingdom, we might regard it as always at hand.

The End

Time won't last. While the writer of Ecclesiastes assures us that everything has its season (Eccles. 3:1–8), a mere season is all it has. History itself, this current of time that provides us with a linear march of events, is not a realm to place our bets on. In his own life on earth, Jesus was poignantly aware at all times of the "hour" when his mortal efforts would come to a close. He knew when the hour hadn't come (John 2:4; 7:6, 8, 30), when it was fast approaching (4:23), and when it arrived in full (5:25; 12:23, 27, 31). Jesus knew that the coming of his hour would mean many things: humiliation and denunciation, anguish and death. As any of us would, he frankly declares when the hour arrives, "Now my soul is troubled." Yet Jesus refuses to say, "Father, save me from this hour," knowing that personal suffering is not the only consequence of this arrival. Jesus understands the meaning of his time on earth far better than most of us: "No, it is for this reason that I have come to this hour. Father, glorify your name" (John 12:27).

The other three Gospels record Passion predictions that demonstrate how Jesus is always moving intentionally toward the cross of sacrifice (e.g., Luke 9:22, 44; 18:31–33). Jesus urges his listeners to learn to read the signs of the times as well, so as not to be caught off guard (Luke 12:54–56; 17:22–37; 21:7–36). In John's Gospel, however, Jesus consciously moves in the direction of glory and fulfillment as he approaches his hour. The discordant notes of self-sacrifice are still heard, but the dominant theme is that Jesus is glory-bound.

In contemplating the element of time across the Gospels, it becomes plain that the day of our salvation is today, the most important moment is now, and the time to act is immediately. This urgency is brought on by the lateness of the hour, which harbors both passion and glory in its arrival. Whether we define this "hour" as the end of the world, our own personal mortality, or the grace implicit in the present moment — and Christianity has considered all these definitions and excludes none of them — we have no time to lose in making our decision.

What decision are we asked to make? To love God and each other. To care for the hungry, thirsty, sick, and isolated. To keep the welfare of our enemies and persecutors in our prayers and intentions. These are simple choices and profound ones. The Gospel is crammed with directives for our conduct and interior attitude and bold examples of how we might live and act and speak — and die. If the Gospels are not enough, the ongoing mission of the church in Acts and in Paul's letters spells out more details and offers yet more advice. The consequences of our decision, for or against the Gospel course, are mythically considered in the final book of the Bible, Revelation. "There will be no more delay," says the voice from heaven, "The mystery of God will be fulfilled" (Rev. 10:6, 7). God *is* the ultimate mystery; but the will of God is not. Those who listen to the divine word cannot plead ignorance to the way.

One blessed assurance regarding time is offered by the second generation of Christians: "Jesus Christ is the same yesterday and today and forever" (Heb. 13:8). If we embrace that truth, time is our friend and eternity our joyful destiny.

Read, Explore, Discuss

Ecclesiastes 3:1–8: For everything, a season

Wisdom 3:1–9: The just will not perish

2 Maccabees 7: Hope in the God of immortality

Mark 9:33–37; 10:13–16: Children and the Kingdom

Matthew 13, 18, 20–22, 25: Kingdom parables

Luke 12:54–56; 17:20–21; 21:5–36: Signs of the times

John 2:4; 4:21–26; 5:25–29; 7:6, 30; 12:20–36; 16:1–33: Knowing the hour

Revelation 7:15–17; 10:5–7; 11:17–18; 12:10–12; 19:5–16: The victory is decided

Revelation 1:8, 17; 3:20; 21:1–8; 22:1–21: God's time and ours

In the Spirit of Responsive Listening

- Consider every day an urgent opportunity to marry the will of God in every decision.

- Become like a child, open to each new person, event, and possibility.

- Live for today. Act for eternity.

Epilogue

S OME READERS WILL FIND this series of five essays on Scripture surprisingly arbitrary, missing crucial elements of our faith, and overlooking passages central to understanding the Jewish and Christian stories. Let me be the first to admit that this would have been a very different book if the chapter titles had been: "Journey," "Justice," "Grace," "Forgiveness," and "Hope." Or any combination of five biblical concepts close to your heart.

So if you feel that something vital is lacking, I thank God for your perception and hope you will finish the job in your own reflection on Scripture. Every book I write ends on a note of self-recrimination, in the sober awareness of all that wasn't said and might have been. The very title of this book, *Listening to God's Word*, anticipates that there's more listening to be done. This work may serve that goal by its method, then, as much as its content. Each chapter models the exploration of one big idea across the Testaments, recognizing that Hebrew and Christian treatments of any subject are both dependent and developed. These chapters also suggest that no idea stands alone: "God" can be understood only in terms of "Creation." "World" is revealed in relationship to God through "Love" and "Sin." Our "Story" is known through a particular "Community" and God's "Promises." The "Crisis" of being can't be examined apart from the accusation and consolation of "prophecy." And "Time" makes no sense, religiously speaking, without its better companion, "Eternity."

What follows are the *Top Ten Things to Remember* as we continue to listen to Scripture faithfully and openly:

1. The Bible is true. Even the parts that never historically happened.

2. Scripture is not the story of God so much as it is the story of God's people.

3. In saying so, we claim the Bible as our story most personally.

4. God's word is a living word, not a record of past events.

5. A living word has the power to speak directly to the present generation and moment.

6. The gracious souls who wrote and compiled the Bible did it not to preserve the past but to rescue the future.

7. In God's opinion, the world is worth rescuing at all costs — even at the price of the cross.

8. The message of God's word, even the book of Revelation, is ultimately hopeful. Why else call it good news?

9. Time is a gift that expires, but it has a window swung wide on eternity.

10. The most important moment in the history of the world is now. It is the only moment in which you and I are free to act.